Baking

• MASTERING THE BASICS •

Baking

Basics to Brilliance
Techniques, Tips and Trusted Recipes

MURDOCH BOOKS

Contents

Introduction

Basics techniques and recipes form the foundations for any cooking style — especially when baking. But successful results can only be achieved if these foundations are strong, well formed and foolproof.

Whether you are a novice cook or a competent baker, this book will teach you how to master the basic techniques and recipes associated with baking. Together with invaluable tips, step-by-step instructions and over 70 fail-safe recipes, *Mastering the Basics: Baking* will give you the confidence needed for success every time you turn on your oven.

From decadent jumbo chocolate fudge cookies and savoury spinach and cheese muffins to well-loved chocolate caramel slice and the best-ever vanilla butter cake, this collection of reliable recipes will provide you with the only baking companion you will ever need.

Baking
Basics

Baking ingredients

Baking powder is a leavener that is used to help aerate mixtures. It is a combination of bicarbonate of soda (baking soda), cream of tartar (or other acidic powder) and usually cornflour (cornstarch) or rice flour (to absorb moisture). To make your own, combine ½ teaspoon cream of tartar, ½ teaspoon cornflour and ¼ teaspoon bicarbonate of soda to replace 1 teaspoon of commercial baking powder.

Bicarbonate of soda, also called baking soda, is not only a component of baking powder but can also be used as a leavener in its own right. It is activated with the aid of an acid, so is therefore used in mixtures with an acidic ingredient such as buttermilk, yoghurt, sour cream, citrus juice and even molasses. It is important to cook these mixtures as soon as possible, because the bicarbonate of soda is activated as soon as it comes into contact with the acidic ingredient — if the mixture is left to sit, it won't rise as much as it should and the end product will have a coarser, more open texture.

Butter adds flavour, shortness/tenderness and colour. When it is beaten, air is incorporated which, in turn, helps leaven baked goods as they cook. It can also be rubbed into flour or melted and mixed with other ingredients. Unsalted butter is sweeter than salted and gives you more control over the amount of salt in your baking — you can add as much as you want. If you are creaming butter, make sure it is softened by standing at room temperature for at least 30 minutes before using. If rubbing into dry ingredients, make sure it is chilled.

Buttermilk, a cultured milk, is made by adding souring agents to milk. It adds a subtle acidity to cakes and batters, such as pancakes, and is used in conjunction with bicarbonate of soda (baking soda), in goods such as soda bread and scones. Its acidity reacts with the alkaline properties of the soda to provide a particularly good lift. To make your own buttermilk, add 1 tablespoon of fresh lemon juice to 300 ml (10½ fl oz) of regular milk.

Cocoa powder is the unsweetened ground powder made from grinding the cocoa solids when the cocoa butter (the fat) is removed from cocoa beans. Sift it before using to remove any lumps. Sweetened cocoa powder is sold as drinking chocolate. Dutch cocoa is considered the best quality cocoa powder, having a rich and intense flavour and a dark colour.

Cornflour, also known as cornstarch, is made from corn or maize (gluten-free) or wheat (labelled as wheaten cornflour). In baking, it is used in small quantities to replace plain (all-purpose) flour to give a lighter texture.

Cream is used sometimes in baked goods to enrich and tenderise. The fat content of cream determines how rich it is and also its whipping characteristics — the higher the fat content, the easier it will be to whip and the thicker it will be when whipped (low-fat cream won't whip at all). Double (thick/heavy) cream has a 48 per cent butter fat content and is the thickest type of cream. Pouring cream, also known as whipping or single cream, has a fat content of 35 per cent. Thickened cream, also known as whipping cream, is pouring cream with gelatine added to thicken it slightly and make it more stable. It is ideal for whipping. Sour cream adds a pleasant acidity, and richness, to dishes.

Eggs enrich, give structure, bind, lighten, tenderise and add flavour to baked goods. Store them, pointed end down, in their original carton in the refrigerator. Bring eggs to room temperature before using — if you're short on time, you can put them in a bowl of lukewarm water for 10 minutes. All the recipes in this book use 59/60 g (2¼ oz) eggs.

Flour provides the basic structure for the majority of baked goods. Self-raising flour is simply plain (all-purpose) flour with baking powder added. To make your own, add 2 teaspoons baking powder to 150 g (5½ oz/1 cup) plain flour and sift several times before using. Honey and golden syrup are used to sweeten baked goods, such as rich hot puddings, tarts, cakes and biscuits.

Milk is often used in cakes, puddings, breads and quick breads to help moisten and bind the dry ingredients, and to prevent the final baked product being heavy and dry. Always use full-cream cow's milk in baking recipes unless otherwise specified.

Oil is often used in recipes that don't rely on air being incorporated into butter by the creaming method. Baked goods made with oil tend to store better and stay moister than those made with butter. Oils used in baking generally have a mild flavour, such as sunflower, vegetable and light olive oils.

Salt is mainly used in baking as a seasoning and flavour enhancer. Always add a little salt (usually about ½ teaspoon) to baked goods if using unsalted butter.

Sugar adds flavour, moisture and tenderness to baked goods. Granulated sugar is the most commonly available, but caster (superfine) sugar, with its fine grains that dissolve

quickly, is a better choice for baking. Icing (confectioners') sugar is powdered white sugar and is available as pure icing sugar or icing sugar mixture, which has a little cornflour (cornstarch) added to prevent lumps. Light brown sugar is fine, granulated sugar with molasses added to enrich the flavour. Dark brown sugar has even more molasses added. To substitute brown sugar for white, or vice versa, measure out the same weight (grams or ounces), rather than volume (cups).

Vanilla is used in various forms. Natural vanilla extract and vanilla essence are concentrated flavours derived from vanilla beans. Buy pure essence or extract and avoid those labelled with 'artificial' or 'imitation' as they don't contain any real vanilla. Thick vanilla bean paste is also available and offers a convenient way of adding vanilla seeds to recipes. If using vanilla beans, wash and dry the pod thoroughly after use and place it in a container of sugar to subtly flavour it.

Baking equipment

Ovens

Not all ovens cook in the same way so it is important to get to know your oven and make your own adjustments to recipes if necessary. Even when an oven is accurately calibrated, its temperature may be slightly out. Use a good-quality oven thermometer to monitor the temperature regularly and make sure the seals are in good order to prevent heat escaping.

Fan-forced or convection ovens, which use a fan to circulate the heat, cook at a higher temperature and more quickly than conventional ovens. The recipes in this book have been tested in conventional ovens — if cooking in a fan-forced oven, decrease the oven temperature by 20°C (68°F) and check regularly towards the end of cooking as the time may need to be reduced by 10–20 per cent. When baking in a conventional oven, place cakes in the centre of the oven and swap multiple trays of biscuits around halfway through cooking to ensure even cooking. If you have two cakes in the oven at once, make sure there is plenty of room between them to allow the heat to circulate evenly.

Measuring

Accurate measuring, whether by weight or volume, is essential for success when baking. Always use one set of measurements when preparing a recipe — metric (grams and ml) or imperial (oz and fl oz) by weighing, or measuring by volume (cups).

Measuring cups are used to measure dry or non-liquid ingredients. They are generally available in plastic or metal and in sets of 60 ml (2 fl oz/¼ cup), 80 ml (2½ fl oz/⅓ cup), 125 ml (4 fl oz/½ cup) and 250 ml (9 fl oz/1 cup) measures. Spoon the ingredient into the cup until heaped, then, without compressing it, run a flat-bladed knife across the top to level. All cup measures in this book are level, not heaped.

Measuring jugs are used to measure liquids. Look for a glass or see-through jug with clear markings and a good spout.

Measuring spoons are used to measure small amounts of both dry and liquid ingredients. They are available in sets that generally include a ¼ teaspoon, ½ teaspoon, 1 teaspoon and 1 tablespoon. One teaspoon equals 5 ml in volume. Tablespoons, however, can come in either 15 ml (½ fl oz/ 3 teaspoon) or 20 ml (¾ fl oz/4 teaspoon) volumes. This book uses 20 ml tablespoons. Check your tablespoon volume and

if you are using a 15 ml tablespoon, add an extra teaspoon for every tablespoon of the ingredient specified in the recipe. This is particularly important for ingredients such as baking powder and bicarbonate of soda (baking soda). All tablespoon and teaspoon measures in this book are level — use a flat-bladed knife to level ingredients, as for cup measures.

Scales, electronic versions in particular, are the most accurate way of measuring dry ingredients, such as flour or sugar, and non-liquid, soft ingredients, such as yoghurt or jam. Electronic scales are now affordable and are an invaluable addition to your kitchen. Most give metric and imperial weights, and let you switch between the two. They may also let you 'zero' the reading so you can measure several ingredients in the same bowl one after another, which is handy for one-bowl mixes.

Mixing

Bowls are fundamental to baking and it is important to have a good selection of sizes. Stainless-steel bowls are versatile and durable and are good conductors of heat and cold. Ceramic and glass bowls are sturdy and are also suitable for heating and melting ingredients. Plastic bowls aren't a good choice for mixing as they absorb flavours and become greasy over time.

Electric mixers offer an easy, efficient way to cream butter and sugar, whisk egg whites and combine batters.

Hand-held electric beaters have detachable beaters and sometimes whisk attachments, and a range of speeds. They are relatively inexpensive, store easily and can be used to whisk or beat mixtures. They are also needed if whisking or beating a mixture over a saucepan of simmering water. However, they aren't suitable for heavy-duty mixing, such as bread doughs, and are not as efficient as the stand versions.

Electric mixers that are mounted on a stand have a bowl that screws into the stand and usually come with a range of attachments such as a beating paddle, whisk and dough hook. Like hand-held beaters, they have a range of speeds, but their motors are more powerful and therefore able to cope with larger and thicker mixtures. Buy the best quality mixer you can afford.

Food processors are invaluable when baking, from finely chopping nuts to making breadcrumbs and even pastry. Buy the best-quality food processor you can afford, and ensure it has a large bowl. A mini food processor that will cope with small quantities is also a good investment.

Bakers' friends

Baking beads/weights are small, re-usable ceramic or metal weights that are used when blind baking pastry. You can use dried beans or rice instead, but proper weights are handy.

Cake testers are thin metal or bamboo skewers. Metal ones are available from kitchenware stores and are the best option as they won't leave large holes in your baking. The skewer is inserted into the centre of a cake and if it's cooked, it will be clean when withdrawn (unless otherwise stated in the recipe).

Large metal spoons are useful for folding dry ingredients into a mixture or folding in whisked egg whites without losing the incorporated air.

Non-stick baking paper or silpat mats can be used to line baking trays as an alternative to greasing and flouring them. Silpat mats are available from speciality kitchenware stores and can be used time and time again. Wash in hot soapy water and dry thoroughly before storing.

Oven thermometers are important kitchen gadgets. Not all ovens are calibrated and are likely to be at least a couple of degrees out. 'Hot spots' are also common. A thermometer will allow you to check if your oven is accurate and adjust the temperature if necessary. Move the thermometer around in the oven when set at the same temperature and note the reading to check if you have any 'hot spots'. There is no need to remove it from your oven between oven uses.

Palette knives can be bought in various sizes and degrees of flexibility. They have a thin, flat blade with a rounded end that makes them useful for transferring biscuits from a tray to a rack, loosening cakes from tins and spreading icing (frosting).

Pastry brushes have natural, nylon or silicone bristles and are used to glaze tarts, brush egg wash onto pastries and doughs, and grease cake tins. Have a few brushes of varying sizes and wash and dry them thoroughly before storing. Avoid cheaper brushes as they tend to shed their bristles.

Piping (icing) bags and nozzles/tips are used to pipe meringue or biscuit mixtures into shapes, to pipe cream, buttercream or other icings (frostings) and to decorate with icing. Various bags and sizes and shapes of nozzles are available. Make sure the bags are cleaned well and dried completely before storing.

Rolling pins should be straight, solid and long enough to roll out a full quantity of pastry or dough without marking the surface with the ends. A good size is about 45 cm (17¾ inches) long and 5 cm (2 inches) in diameter. Wood is preferable to ceramic or marble, as it can hold a fine layer of flour on its surface that will help prevent the pastry or dough sticking. The best ones are made of hard wood with a close grain and very smooth finish. Clean it by wiping with a damp cloth — never immerse a wooden rolling pin in water.

Ruler Keep a ruler or measuring tape in your utensil drawer for checking tin or cutter dimensions, lining tins and checking the thickness of pastry or biscuit doughs.

Saucepans and frying pans are great supportive equipment when baking. They are used for everything from making melt-and-mix cakes, melting chocolate, making caramel, cooking syrups and sauces, and poaching fruit. Have a selection of different sizes for a variety of uses.

Sieves are used to sift flour to help incorporate air, to combine ingredients evenly, such as flour and cocoa powder or baking powder, and to dust flour onto a work surface before rolling out pastry or kneading dough. They are also used to dust icing (confectioners') sugar or cocoa over baked goods.

Spatulas can be made of silicone, rubber or plastic. Silicone and rubber ones are more flexible, however rubber ones tend to absorb colours and flavours more readily. Spatulas are used to fold and combine mixtures and scrape them from bowls, blenders and food processors. Have a few different sizes and shapes for various tasks.

Timers are necessary for accurate timing and to prevent food burning. Digital timers are more accurate than mechanical ones. Many ovens have inbuilt timers.

Whisks are used to incorporate air into a mixture, remove lumps and combine liquid mixtures, such as eggs and oil. They come in all shapes and sizes — a large and small wire balloon whisk will usually cover all required tasks.

Wooden spoons are used to mix, beat and stir. They are particularly good for mixtures being heated in a saucepan and 'heavier' mixtures that require stirring or beating.

Cutting and grating

Graters come in many different shapes and sizes, from the traditional box grater to rasp-shaped Microplanes. They have various perforations of different sizes designed for specific uses, from finely grating citrus zest and nutmeg to coarsely grating chocolate and cheese. Look for a grater with a variety of perforations or have a couple on hand for different tasks.

Knives should be sharpened regularly and washed by hand (rather than putting them in the dishwasher) to help retain their sharpness and to prevent chipping of the blade. Make sure they are always dried thoroughly before storing. An all-purpose cook's knife is handy for chopping ingredients such as chocolate, nuts and dried fruits. A paring knife can be used to trim pastry, cut fruit and make small incisions. A long serrated knife is best for cutting cakes into even layers (see page 25), slicing biscotti between bakings, and cutting cake and bread into portions.

Biscuit and pastry cutters also come in a variety of shapes and sizes, from simple plain and fluted rounds to more intricate designs such as numbers, letters and novelty shapes. Metal cutters generally have a better edge than plastic ones, giving a cleaner cut without having to apply much pressure. A pastry wheel with a fluted edge is also a handy tool for cutting biscuits and pastry. Wash and dry cutters thoroughly before storing. (Metal ones are best dried in a low oven.)

Scissors are another useful utensil when baking, for tasks such as cutting out non-stick baking paper when lining cake tins and snipping pastry for decorations. It is a good idea to have a good-quality pair in the kitchen to use solely for cooking.

Bakeware

Baking trays Choose the largest trays that will fit in your oven and make sure they are solid so they don't buckle. Have two or more trays so you can cook a few batches at once.

Cake and loaf (bar) tins come in various sizes, shapes and finishes. It is important to use the size and shape specified in the recipe or the outcome of your baking may be affected. The type of metal that tins are made from and their finish will affect the way they conduct heat and therefore cook. Shiny bakeware will deflect heat and prevent scorching, whereas dark, matt, non-stick bakeware will absorb and hold heat more readily, giving a darker, slightly thicker, crust. Choose good-quality tins, preferably with straight sides, and prepare them as instructed. (see pages 22-23). All the tins in this book have been measured at the base, with the exception of kugelhopf tins, which are best measured across the top. If a tin is marked with a diameter measurement, measure it to ensure it's correct (there are a number of spring-form tins available, for example, that are incorrectly marked).

Dariole moulds and ramekins are mostly available in metal or ceramic form and are used to make individual cakes and puddings.

Muffin tins generally come in three sizes – Texas or large (250 ml/9 fl oz/1 cup), medium (80 ml/2½ fl oz/⅓ cup) and mini (20 ml/¾ fl oz/1 tablespoon).

Patty pan tins are used to make cupcakes and other small cakes. They have either a flat or rounded base.

Pie and tart (flan) tins come in a range of shapes, sizes, depths and finishes. They often don't need greasing before using as the pastry's high butter content prevents it sticking. Tart tins with removable bases ('loose-based') are often used as they allow tarts to be removed easily. Like all cake tins, pie and tart tins should be cleaned in hot soapy water and dried thoroughly (preferably in a low oven) before storing.

Ring, kugelhopf and angel food cake tins have a central tube, which forms the cake or bread mixture into a ring shape that enables it to cook relatively quickly and evenly. Ring and kugelhopf tins can't be lined so it is best to grease them well and lightly dust with flour (if specified in the recipe), as detailed on page 22. Angel food cake tins don't need to be greased, lined or floured.

Spring-form tins have a removable base that is released when a sprung latch on the side is opened. You will need to use a spring-form tin when making delicate cakes, such as flourless ones, or cheesecakes that can't be upturned onto a wire rack. Make sure the latch is strong so the base and side fit snugly together — this will prevent any leaking. Turning the base upside down before locking it in place will create a base without a lip, which will make removing the cake easier.

Freezing

Most baked goods can be frozen for up to 3 months. Unfilled and/or un-iced cakes, biscuits, slices, quick breads, breads and tarts freeze better than those with decorations and/or fillings. Cakes and biscuits decorated with fondant, glacé or royal icing; cheesecakes; baked goods that are meringue-based; and recipes with cream-based fillings will not freeze well.

Before you wrap baked goods for freezing, always make sure they have cooled completely. Then, wrap them well in plastic wrap before sealing in a double layer of foil, a freezer bag or a snap-lock bag (make sure you expel as much air as possible) to prevent them losing moisture while in the freezer. Small baked goods, such as biscuits, slices and cupcakes, can be placed in an airtight container, layered with freezer wrap or non-stick baking paper, and then sealed. Label and date clearly before putting them in the freezer.

Uncooked pastry (see pages 16-21) and biscuit doughs without a leavening agent can also be frozen successfully. Shape, roll or cut biscuit dough and freeze on baking trays. Once frozen, pack into airtight containers, separated by freezer wrap or non-stick baking paper, or in freezer bags. Bake the biscuits straight from the freezer, adding about 5 minutes extra to the cooking time.

Thaw other baked goods at room temperature or in the fridge and bring to room temperature before serving. Try to avoid thawing them in the microwave, as they can defrost unevenly and 'toughen' in the process.

Basic mixing techniques

Melt & mix *(cakes, biscuits, slices, quick breads)*

This is the quickest and easiest method for combining ingredients.

1 Mix the dry ingredients together and then make a well in the centre.

2 Melt the butter (and other ingredients, as instructed) and cool, if specified. Pour the wet ingredients into the well in the dry ingredients and use a wooden spoon to stir until well combined. This can also be done in a food processor, using the pulse button.

Creaming *(cakes, biscuits, slices)*

The creaming method is used to beat butter and sugar with an electric mixer (although you can do it with a wooden spoon and a lot of muscle) to change the consistency of the mixture, incorporate air and, in turn, help the cake, biscuits or slice rise slightly during baking.

1 The butter should be softened, but not melted. Combine the butter, sugar and any specified flavourings (such as vanilla or grated citrus zest) in a suitable-sized mixing bowl.

2 Use an electric mixer to beat the ingredients. For best results, don't take shortcuts — keep beating until the mixture is creamy, increased slightly in volume and paler in colour. The sugar should have almost dissolved. Other ingredients will now be either beaten, stirred or folded in before baking.

Rubbing in *(biscuits, slices, scones, quick breads, pastry)*

Rubbing in should be done quickly and lightly, so the butter doesn't melt. It helps if your hands are cool — run them under cold water on a hot day if necessary.

1 The butter is usually chilled, but not always, for this method. Cut it into small, even-sized pieces.

2 Use your fingertips to rub the butter into the dry ingredients until the mixture resembles fine or coarse breadcrumbs, as specified. (This method can also be done in a food processor, using the pulse button.) Other ingredients are usually stirred in after this, using a flat-bladed knife or wooden spoon.

Folding *(cakes, meringue mixtures)*

Folding involves incorporating one mixture into another. It is often used to combine a light, aerated mixture (such as whisked egg whites) with a heavier mixture (such as melted chocolate and butter) or when flour is incorporated into a creamed butter mixture so as not to toughen it before baking.

1 Add the lighter mixture to the heavier mixture in batches. Use a large metal spoon or spatula to cut through the centre, then turn the spoon and draw it up around the side of the bowl.

2 Give the bowl a turn and repeat the folding, making sure you reach right down to the base of the bowl so the mixtures are evenly combined and there are no pockets of either mixture left. Fold until the mixtures are just combined. Do not beat or stir at any stage, as incorporated air will be lost and/or the mixture will toughen.

Whisking *(cakes, meringue mixtures)*

This technique is used when the recipe requires air to be incorporated into eggs or egg whites. Eggs and egg whites should be at room temperature, as this enables them to hold more air than when they are chilled. Use a mixing bowl that is clean, dry and the appropriate size for the quantity of eggs or egg whites to be whisked. Use an electric mixer with a whisk attachment for the greatest efficiency, though a balloon whisk can also be used if you prefer.

Eggs and sugar

1 When whisking eggs with sugar, such as for the base for a sponge cake, whisk until the mixture has increased in volume and is very thick and pale. The recipe will usually specify that the mixture needs to be whisked until a ribbon trail forms when the whisk is lifted. This method is sometimes done in a bowl over a saucepan of simmering water so the eggs cook and thicken while being whisked.

Egg whites

2 When whisking egg whites, for a cake or to make meringue, whisk until soft or firm peaks form, depending on the recipe.

3 If whisking in sugar, add it gradually, a spoonful at a time, while whisking constantly. Continue whisking until all the sugar has been incorporated, the mixture is very thick and glossy and the sugar has dissolved. You can check this by rubbing a small amount of the mixture between your fingers.

Icings

Vanilla buttercream

PREPARATION TIME 5 minutes
COOKING TIME nil
MAKES about 1 cup, enough
for 12 cupcakes or a 22 cm
(8½ inch) cake

....

100 g (3½ oz) unsalted butter,
  softened slightly
1 teaspoon natural vanilla extract
160 g (5¾ oz/1⅓ cups) icing
  (confectioners') sugar, sifted
Milk (optional)

1 Use an electric mixer to beat the
butter and vanilla in a small bowl until
pale and creamy (*pic 1*).

2 Gradually beat in the icing sugar,
about 60 g (2¼ oz/½ cup) at a time,
until well combined (*pic 2*).

3 Test the consistency (*pic 3*). If the
buttercream is too thick, beat in a little
milk, 1 teaspoon at a time, until it
reaches the desired consistency.

VARIATIONS
Chocolate buttercream: Sift the
icing sugar with 30 g (1 oz/¼ cup)
unsweetened cocoa powder.
Makes about 1¼ cups.

White chocolate buttercream: Beat in
50 g (1¾ oz) white chocolate, melted
and cooled, after adding the icing
sugar. Makes about 1¼ cups.

Orange buttercream: Omit the vanilla.
Fold in ½ teaspoon finely grated orange
zest after adding the icing sugar.

Maple buttercream: Reduce the icing
sugar to 150 g (5½ oz/1¼ cups). Beat
in 2 tablespoons maple syrup after
adding the icing sugar.

Hazelnut buttercream: Replace
20 g (¾ oz) of the butter with
80 g (2¾ oz/¼ cup) chocolate
hazelnut spread. Reduce the icing
sugar to 150 g (5½ oz/1¼ cups). Beat
in 1 tablespoon Frangelico (hazelnut
liqueur) after adding the icing sugar.

Citrus buttercream: Beat in 2 teaspoons
finely grated lemon or orange zest after
adding the icing sugar. Tint with yellow
or orange food colouring, if desired.

Coffee buttercream: Dissolve
1 teaspoon instant coffee granules in
1 teaspoon boiling water, then cool.
Beat into the buttercream after adding
the icing sugar.

Raspberry jam buttercream: Omit
the vanilla. Fold in 1½ tablespoons
raspberry jam (not a reduced-sugar
variety) after adding the icing sugar.

Nut buttercream: Omit the vanilla.
Fold in 1½ tablespoons very finely
chopped pistachios or roasted, skinned
hazelnuts after adding the icing sugar.

Spiced buttercream: Omit the vanilla.
Fold in ½ teaspoon ground cinnamon
or mixed (pumpkin pie) spice after
adding the icing sugar.

Glacé icing

PREPARATION TIME 5 minutes
COOKING TIME 2 minutes
MAKES about ¾ cup, enough
for 12 cupcakes or a 22 cm
(8½ inch) cake

....

180 g (6¼ oz/1½ cups) icing
  (confectioners') sugar, sifted
20 g (¾ oz) unsalted butter
  1 tablespoon water

1 Put all the ingredients in a
heatproof bowl over a saucepan of
simmering water (make sure the water
doesn't touch the base of the bowl)
(*pic 1*).

2 Stir until the butter has melted
and the icing (frosting) is glossy and
smooth (*pic 2*). Use immediately.

VARIATIONS
Citrus glacé icing: Replace the water
with 1 tablespoon orange, lemon or
lime juice and add 1 teaspoon finely

grated orange, lemon or lime zest.
Tint with yellow, orange or green
food colouring, if desired.

Coffee glacé icing: Replace the water
with 1 teaspoon instant coffee
granules mixed with 1 tablespoon
boiling water.

Chocolate glacé icing: Add
2 tablespoons sifted unsweetened
cocoa powder with the icing sugar and
increase the water to 2 tablespoons.

1 Beat the butter and vanilla in a small bowl until pale and creamy.

2 Gradually beat in the icing sugar until the mixture is well combined.

3 Use a flat-bladed or palette knife to test whether the buttercream is a spreadable consistency.

TIP This buttercream and all the variations can be kept, covered, in the refrigerator for up to 30 minutes before using. If storing for any longer, set aside at room temperature to soften before using. The texture and consistency of the buttercreams will be affected if refrigerated for more than 30 minutes.

1 Put the icing sugar, butter and water in a bowl over a saucepan of simmering water.

2 The icing is ready to use when the butter has melted and the mixture is glossy and smooth.

Shortcrust pastry

A very high butter content and the addition of egg yolk gives shortcrust pastry and sweet shortcrust pastry the characteristic melt-in-the-mouth texture and rich flavour. These pastries aren't difficult to master, but there are a few basic rules to note when making them. The pastry should be kept as cool as possible at every stage of the process — if it becomes too warm at any point, the finished result will be heavy and greasy. The pastry will also become difficult to work with if it becomes too warm. As with all pastries, care must be taken not to overwork it when mixing and rolling out or it may shrink and toughen during cooking. Always rest the finished pastry in the refrigerator before rolling it out and again when it is in the tin(s) before baking. This assists in preventing shrinkage and toughening of the pastry.

1 With your palms facing upwards, use your fingertips to rub in the butter so you can lift and aerate the flour mixture.

2 Use a flat-bladed knife to gradually incorporate the liquid ingredients into the dry ingredients until a coarse dough forms.

3 Knead the dough lightly, just a few times, until it is smooth.

4 Shape the dough into a disc and wrap in plastic wrap.

Shortcrust pastry

PREPARATION TIME 10 minutes
(+ 30 minutes chilling)
MAKES enough to line a shallow
24 cm (9½ inch) fluted tart (flan)
tin or four 8 cm (3¼ inch) fluted
tart tins

260 g (9¼ oz/1¾ cups) plain
  (all-purpose) flour
½ teaspoon salt
125 g (4½ oz) chilled unsalted
  butter, diced
1 egg yolk
2 teaspoons lemon juice
1 tablespoon chilled water,
  approximately

1 Sift the flour and salt together into
a large bowl. With your palms facing
upwards, use your fingertips to rub in
the butter, lifting the flour mixture up
as you rub to aerate it, until the mixture
resembles fine breadcrumbs (*pic 1*).

2 Make a well in the centre of the
dry ingredients. Whisk together the
egg yolk, lemon juice and water. Add
to the dry ingredients and use a flat-
bladed knife to gradually incorporate
until a coarse dough forms, adding a
little more water if necessary (*pic 2*).

3 Press the dough together — it
should be soft, but not sticky. Turn it
out onto a lightly floured, cool work
surface and lightly knead just a few

times, until the dough is smooth
(*pic 3*).

4 Shape the dough into a disc and
then wrap in plastic wrap (*pic 4*).
Place in the refrigerator for 30 minutes
to rest before rolling out and using
as desired.

VARIATIONS
Parmesan shortcrust pastry: After
rubbing in butter, add 35 g (1¼ oz/
⅓ cup) finely grated parmesan cheese.

Herb shortcrust pastry: After rubbing
in the butter, add 1 tablespoon finely
chopped chives and 1 tablespoon
finely chopped basil leaves.

Sweet shortcrust pastry

PREPARATION TIME 10 minutes
(+ 30 minutes chilling)
MAKES enough to line a shallow
24 cm (9½ inch) fluted tart (flan)
tin, four 8 cm (3¼ inch) fluted
tart tins or 24 patty pan holes

225 g (8 oz/1½ cups) plain
  (all-purpose) flour
30 g (1 oz/¼ cup) icing
  (confectioners') sugar
½ teaspoon salt
125 g (4½ oz) chilled unsalted
  butter, cubed
1 egg, lightly whisked
Chilled water (optional)

1 Sift the flour, icing sugar and
salt together into a large bowl. With
your palms facing upwards, use your
fingertips to rub in the butter, lifting
the flour mixture up as you rub to
aerate it, until the mixture resembles
fine breadcrumbs (*pic 1*).

2 Make a well in the centre of the
dry ingredients. Add the whisked
egg and use a flat-bladed knife to
gradually incorporate until a coarse
dough forms, adding a little water
if necessary (*pic 2*).

3 Press the dough together — it
should be soft, but not sticky. Turn
it out onto a lightly floured, cool work
surface and lightly knead a few times,
until the dough is smooth (*pic 3*).

4 Shape the dough into a disc
and then wrap in plastic wrap
(*pic 4*). Place in the refrigerator for
30 minutes to rest before rolling
out and using as desired.

VARIATIONS
Almond shortcrust pastry: Replace
75 g (2¾ oz/½ cup) of the flour with
50 g (1¾ oz/½ cup) almond meal and
reduce the butter to 100 g (3½ oz).

Brown sugar shortcrust pastry:
Replace the icing sugar with 65 g
(2¼ oz/⅓ cup, lightly packed)
light brown sugar.

TIP Both shortcrust pastries can be made up to 3 days in advance and stored, wrapped in plastic wrap, in the refrigerator.
Set aside at room temperature to soften slightly before rolling out. Uncooked pastry can be frozen, wrapped well in plastic wrap
and then sealed in a freezer bag, for up to 4 weeks. Place it in the refrigerator to thaw completely, rather than leaving it out at
room temperature.

Making shortcrust pastry in the food processor

PREPARATION TIME 10 minutes
(+ 30 minutes chilling)
MAKES enough to line a shallow 24 cm
(9½ inch) fluted tart (flan) tin or four
8 cm (3¼ inch) fluted tart tins

....

260 g (9¼ oz/1¾ cups) plain
   (all-purpose) flour
½ teaspoon salt
125 g (4½ oz) chilled unsalted
   butter, diced
1 egg yolk

2 teaspoons lemon juice
1 tablespoon chilled water,
   approximately

1   Put the flour, salt and butter in a
food processor and process until the
mixture resembles coarse breadcrumbs
(*pic 1*).

2   Add the egg yolk, lemon juice
and water and use the pulse button
to process briefly until the dough just
starts to cling together, adding a little

more chilled water to the dough
if necessary (*pic 2*).

3   Press the dough together — it
should be soft, but not sticky. Turn it
out onto a lightly floured, cool work
surface and lightly knead a few times,
just until the dough is smooth.

4   Shape the dough into a disc and
then wrap in plastic wrap. Place in
the refrigerator for 30 minutes to rest
before rolling out and using as desired.

Rolling out shortcrust pastry

1   Remove the pastry from the
refrigerator and, if necessary, set
aside at room temperature for
20–30 minutes or until it is slightly
pliable so it can be rolled out easily.
Lightly flour a rolling pin and work
surface (preferably a cool one, such as
a slab of marble, to prevent the pastry
becoming too warm). Always roll
from the centre of the pastry out to
the edges and in the same direction,
turning the pastry regularly to ensure
it is rolled evenly and doesn't stick
to the work surface. Roll until the
pastry is the desired thickness, usually
3–5 mm (⅛–¼ inch) (*pic 1*).

2   It is not necessary to grease a tart
(flan) tin when baking shortcrust
pastry, even if it's not a non-stick one,
as the high butter content in the pastry
will prevent it sticking. The easiest
way to transfer the rolled dough to
the tin is to carefully, and loosely,
roll it around the rolling pin and lift
it over the tin, then carefully unroll it
(*pic 2*). If using small individual tins,
cut a suitable-sized portion of the
dough before rolling it around the
rolling pin.

3   Use your fingers to carefully press
the pastry into the base and side of the
tin, making sure it is pressed right into
the base edge (*pic 3*).

4   Use the rolling pin to roll over the
top of the tin to trim the excess pastry
(*pic 4*). Alternatively, use a small sharp
knife to cut outwards along the edge
of the tart to trim any excess pastry.

1 Process the flour, salt and butter until the mixture resembles coarse breadcrumbs.

2 Add the egg yolk, lemon juice and water and pulse just until the dough starts to cling together.

1 Always roll from the centre of the pastry out to the edges and in the same direction. Turn the pastry often to ensure it's rolled evenly.

2 Carefully and loosely roll the pastry around the rolling pin and lift it over the tin, then carefully unroll it.

3 Use your fingers to carefully press the pastry into the base and side of the tin, making sure it's pressed right into the base edge.

4 Roll the rolling pin over the top of the tin to trim the excess pastry.

Blind baking

Shortcrust pastry shells need to be partially or completely cooked before the filling is added to make them crisp and prevent them becoming soggy once the filling is added. The technique used for this is called 'blind baking'. The uncooked pastry shell is covered with a piece of non-stick baking paper and then filled with ceramic or metal baking beads (raw rice or dried beans can also be used). The weight of the beads prevents the base from puffing and the sides from slumping during cooking. Whether the pastry is partially or completely cooked depends on the filling you are going to add. Moist fillings that will be baked in the pastry shell (such as baked custard-based fillings or frangipane) require the pastry to be partially cooked. Fillings that won't be baked (such as pastry cream) need to go into pastry shells that have been completely cooked and cooled.

1   Chill the prepared pastry shell until firm — this helps prevent shrinkage during baking. Place the pastry-lined tin on a baking tray. Preheat the oven to 220°C (425°F/ Gas 7) or as specified.

2   Take a square of non-stick baking paper large enough to cover the base and sides of the shell generously. Fold it in half twice, so you end up with a small square. Fold the square in half diagonally to make a triangle, then again to make a thin triangle with a tail. Cut the tail off, then open it

out — you should have an octagon about 5 cm (2 inches) larger than the diameter of the tin. Place it inside the pastry shell to cover, pressing it gently into the edge of the tin (*pic 1*).

3   Fill the pastry shell three-quarters full with baking beads, raw rice or dried beans to weigh the pastry down, making sure they reach right to the sides (*pic 2*).

4   Bake the shell in the preheated oven for 10 minutes. Reduce the oven temperature to 190°C (375°F/

Gas 5), or as instructed in the recipe, and bake for a further 5 minutes or until the pastry is partially cooked and pale gold. Lift out the paper and weights (*pic 3*). Use the pastry shell as directed.

5   If cooking the shell completely, return it to the oven and cook for a further 8–12 minutes or until golden and cooked through (*pic 4*). Set aside on a wire rack until cooled before removing from the tin and filling.

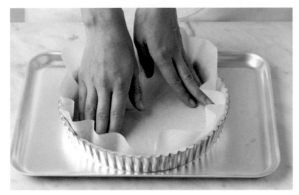

1 Open out the paper octagon and place it inside the pastry shell to cover, pressing it gently into the edges of the tin.

2 Fill the pastry shell three-quarters full with baking beads.

3 Remove the beads from the pastry shell by lifting out the paper.

4 If cooking the shell completely, it needs to be golden and cooked through. Cool it completely in the tin before filling.

Preparing cake tins

Greasing, lining and dusting with flour

The best way to grease a tin is by using a pastry brush to apply melted butter or oil evenly, and not too thickly, over the base and sides. Vegetable oil sprays can also be used.

Non-stick baking paper is excellent for lining cake tins and doesn't need to be greased before you add the cake batter.

Patty pan and muffin tins can be lined with paper cases, which will prevent the mixture sticking while also providing a convenient and attractive case.

Sometimes a recipe asks for a cake tin to be dusted lightly with flour after greasing, instead of lining with paper. To do this, add a spoonful of flour to the tin and then carefully tilt the tin until the flour evenly coats the base and sides, then tap out any excess. Bundt and kugelhopf tins need to be greased and sometimes lightly floured as they can't, for obvious reasons, be lined with non-stick baking paper.

Always follow the instructions for each recipe as to how the tin (or tins) needs to be prepared.

Butter cakes and chocolate cakes

You can usually get away with greasing the tin and lining just the base, but it's better to line both the base and side.

Sponge cakes

Grease the tin, line the base with non-stick baking paper and then dust the whole tin with flour.

Rich fruit cakes

When baking rich fruit cakes, the tins need to have the base and side/s lined with a double thickness of paper and they also need a collar to give extra protection during the long cooking.

1   To make the collar, cut a double strip of baking paper long enough to fit around the outside of the tin and wide enough to extend at least 5 cm (2 inches) above the top.

2   For added protection from the heat, wrap layers of newspaper around the outside of the tin, and then sit the tin on layers of newspaper or an old magazine on a baking tray. The oven temperature when cooking rich fruit cakes is low enough to make this safe.

Lining round tins

1   Put the tin on non-stick baking paper, draw around it and cut out as marked. Cut a strip of baking paper the same length as the tin's circumference and about 5 cm (2 inches) wider than the height. Fold down a cuff, about 2 cm (¾ inch), along one edge and cut it diagonally at 2 cm intervals.

2   Grease the tin. Place the baking paper strip in the tin with the cuff on the base. The diagonal cuts on the cuff will act like pleats and sit neatly on the base. Press the paper onto the base and side, then place the round of baking paper on the base over the pleats.

Lining square tins

Lining a square cake tin is similar to lining a round tin, but simpler. Put the tin on non-stick baking paper, draw around it, then cut out as marked. Cut a strip of baking paper the same length as the circumference of the tin and about 3 cm (1¼ inches) wider than the height. Grease the tin. Place the square of paper in the base and press the strip onto the sides.

Lining Swiss roll (jelly roll) tins

1   Put the tin on non-stick baking paper and draw around it. Measure the tin's depth, add 2 cm (¾ inch), then cut out at that distance from the drawn lines all around. Crease the paper along the lines, then cut from each corner to the drawn corner.

2   Lightly grease the tin. Press the paper into the tin, fitting it neatly into the corners. This method can also be used for lining a slice tin.

Handling cakes

Removing cakes from tins

Some cakes, such as angel food cakes, are left to cool in the tin completely so they don't shrink or collapse. Rich fruit cakes are also left to cool in the tin to keep them moist. However, most cakes are only left in the tin for a few minutes after removing from the oven to allow them to settle and pull away from the sides of the tin a little. They then need to be turned out (or unclipped if using a spring-form tin) to allow the steam to escape while they cool, preventing them from becoming soggy. Whisked cakes, such as sponges, are a little more delicate than creamed cakes, such as butter cakes or pound cakes, so they require a little more care when being turned out of the tin.

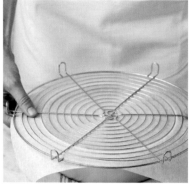

1   First, run a small palette or flat-bladed knife around the outside of the cake, as close to the tin as possible so you don't cut into the side of the cake.

2   Place a wire rack, covered with a tea towel (dish towel) or non-stick baking paper to prevent it marking the cake, on top of the tin.

3   Invert the cake onto the rack and remove any paper stuck to the base of the cake so that the steam can escape and the bottom of the cake won't become soggy.

4   Use a second wire rack to invert the cake the right way up and cool to room temperature before decorating or cutting.

TIP Delicate cakes, such as those made without flour, or cheesecakes that are too fragile to turn upside down when removing from the tin, are best made in a spring-form tin. To remove cakes from spring-form tins, leave the cake in the tin for 5–10 minutes after removing from the oven, then run a small palette or flat-bladed knife around the outside of the cake, as close to the tin as possible. Release the clip on the side of the tin and remove the side. Use 2 egg flips or large palette knives to transfer the cake from the base of the tin to a wire rack to cool. If the cake is very delicate, it is best to allow it to cool on the base of the tin, standing on a wire rack.

Cutting cakes into even layers

Cutting cakes into horizontal layers can be a challenge, but a little forward planning will give you a good success rate. You'll need a ruler, some toothpicks and a long serrated knife.

1   Using a ruler as a guide, insert toothpicks around the outside of the cake to indicate where the cake is to be cut, making sure the layers are an even thickness. The height of the cake will usually determine how many layers it can be cut into. Layers less than 2 cm (¾ inch) high will be hard to cut evenly.

2   Place your hand lightly on top of the cake to hold it steady and use a long serrated knife (if it's longer than the diameter of the cake it will be easier to use) to cut the top layer from the cake, using the toothpicks as a guide.

3   Use the base of a tart (flan) tin, a large spatula or an egg flip to carefully lift the top layer from the cake and set it aside. Repeat to cut any remaining layers.

Rolling a Swiss roll (jelly roll)

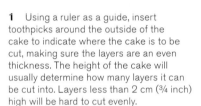

1   Sprinkle a sheet of non-stick baking paper slightly larger than the cake with sugar, icing (confectioners') sugar or cocoa, depending on the recipe. This will coat the outside of the roll and prevent it sticking to the paper. Turn the cake out onto the paper and remove the paper that was lining the tin.

2   Use the paper underneath the cake to help you roll up the cake. Depending on the type of cake, recipes will direct you to either leave the cake rolled up, unroll and re-roll it several times, or unroll it and leave it to cool covered with a slightly damp tea towel (dish towel) to keep it moist.

3   If the cake is cooled while rolled up, unroll it, still on the paper. Use a palette knife to spread the cake with filling. Then, using the paper as a guide, roll it up as tightly as possible. Wrap the paper around it to hold its shape and place on a tray, seam side down. Chill before serving, if directed.

Secrets to a successful meringue

Here are the 10 commandments that will ensure your meringues are crisp, light and snowy white every time.

1 Moisture is meringue's greatest enemy. Cool, dry days are best for making meringues, not humid and/or rainy ones. Moisture in the air will prevent them drying completely and can make them 'weep' during or after cooking.

2 Egg whites at room temperature are best for making meringue as they are able to hold more air than cold ones. However, eggs are easier to separate if cold so it is a good idea to separate them straight from the refrigerator, then leave them at room temperature for 30 minutes or so before using.

3 Separate eggs one at a time into a small ramekin and then transfer to the mixing bowl. This way, if a yolk breaks into the white you only lose that one egg, rather than ruining all the whites you've already separated.

4 Always ensure your equipment is totally clean and dry when whisking egg whites. Even a speck of fat, such as egg yolk, or a drop of moisture in the bowl or on the whisk attachment will inhibit the ability of the egg whites to hold air and therefore produce good volume.

5 A pinch of salt or cream of tartar added to the egg whites before beginning to whisk will help stabilise them.

6 When starting to whisk the egg whites, do it slowly on low or medium speed until soft peaks form.

7 Add the sugar a spoonful at a time and then whisk until combined. The sugar should be added gradually, but there is no need to whisk for an extended amount of time after each addition. It doesn't need to be completely dissolved before the next spoonful is added.

8 Once all the sugar has been added, increase the speed to high and whisk for 2–3 minutes, until all the sugar has dissolved and the mixture is very thick and glossy. A long trailing peak will form when the whisk is lifted. The best way to test if the sugar has dissolved is to rub a little of the mixture between your thumb and finger.

9 Don't overwork the mixture. Once the sugar has dissolved and the mixture is thick and glossy, stop whisking. If the mixture is whisked too much, the meringue will collapse during cooking and beads of sugar will form on the surface.

10 Often the oven is preheated at a slightly higher temperature and then reduced once the meringue goes in. The initial higher temperature will set the outside of the meringue and then the lower temperature will dry the mixture out without colouring it.

Biscuits & Meringues

Jumbo chocolate fudge cookies

The name says it all. These biscuits are big, decadent and totally irresistible. They'll be a sure-fire success at a kid's party, will win over guests at afternoon tea and are sure to satisfy sweet cravings. You can replace the white chocolate with roughly chopped walnuts or macadamia nuts if you like.

MAKES about 18   **PREPARATION TIME** 15 minutes (+ 10 minutes cooling)   **COOKING TIME** 12 minutes

225 g (8 oz/1½ cups) plain (all-purpose) flour
80 g (2¾ oz/¾ cup) unsweetened cocoa powder
285 g (10¼ oz/1½ cups, lightly packed) light brown sugar
180 g (6¼ oz) unsalted butter, chopped
300 g (10½ oz) dark chocolate, chopped
3 eggs, at room temperature, lightly whisked
75 g (2¾ oz/½ cup) chopped white chocolate

1   Preheat the oven to 180°C (350°F/ Gas 4). Line two large baking trays with non-stick baking paper.

2   Sift the flour and cocoa together into a large bowl. Stir in the sugar and make a well in the centre.

3   Put the butter and half the dark chocolate in a small heatproof bowl over a saucepan of simmering water (make sure the base of the bowl doesn't touch the water). Stir over

low heat until the mixture is melted and smooth *(pic 1)*. Remove from the heat and set aside for 10 minutes or until lukewarm.

4   Add the chocolate mixture and egg to the dry ingredients and use a wooden spoon to stir until evenly combined. Stir in the remaining dark and white chocolate *(pic 2)*.

5   Roll 2 tablespoons of mixture into a ball and place on a lined tray. Repeat with the remaining mixture, leaving about 7 cm (2¾ inches) between each ball to allow for spreading. Flatten the balls slightly with your fingertips *(pic 3)*.

6   Bake the biscuits for 12 minutes, swapping the trays around halfway through cooking. Leave the biscuits on the trays for 5 minutes before transferring to a wire rack to cool.

1

2

3

TIP Keep in an airtight container for up to 1 week.

Gingernuts

These delicious biscuits, also called ginger snaps or ginger biscuits, are popular in a number of countries so there are many different versions of the recipe. This one produces crunchy biscuits with an intense ginger flavour that are perfect for dunking in tea or coffee.

MAKES about 35   **PREPARATION TIME** 15 minutes   **COOKING TIME** 15 minutes

300 g (10½ oz/2 cups) plain
   (all-purpose) flour
½ teaspoon bicarbonate of soda
   (baking soda)
1 tablespoon ground ginger
½ teaspoon mixed (pumpkin pie)
   spice
220 g (7¾ oz/1 cup, firmly packed)
   light brown sugar
125 g (4½ oz) chilled unsalted butter,
   chopped
60 ml (2 fl oz/¼ cup) boiling water
1 tablespoon golden syrup
   (light treacle)

1   Preheat the oven to 180°C (350°F/ Gas 4). Line two large baking trays with non-stick baking paper.

2   Sift the flour, bicarbonate of soda, ginger and mixed spice together into a large bowl. Stir in the sugar. Add the butter and use your fingertips to rub it in until the mixture is fine and crumbly *(pic 1)*.

3   Combine the water and golden syrup and stir well. Add to the flour mixture and use a flat-bladed knife to mix to a soft dough *(pic 2)*.

4   Roll 2 teaspoons of mixture into a ball and place on a lined tray. Repeat with the remaining mixture, leaving about 5 cm (2 inches) between each ball to allow for spreading. Use the base of a glass to flatten them slightly *(pic 3)*.

5   Bake the gingernuts for 15 minutes, swapping the trays around halfway through cooking, or until golden and cooked through. Leave on the trays for 10 minutes before transferring to a wire rack to cool completely.

1

2

3

TIPS To ice (frost), combine 60 g (2¼ oz/½ cup) sifted icing (confectioners') sugar, 10 g (¼ oz) melted butter and 2–3 teaspoons lemon juice and spread over the cooled biscuits.
   Keep in an airtight container for up to 1 week.

Simple biscuits

MAKES about 50   **PREPARATION TIME** 30 minutes   **COOKING TIME** 10–15 minutes per batch

125 g (4½ oz) unsalted butter, softened
110 g (3¾ oz/½ cup) caster (superfine) sugar
1 egg
¼ teaspoon natural vanilla extract
150 g (5½ oz/1 cup) plain (all-purpose) flour
150 g (5½ oz/1 cup) self-raising flour
1 quantity filling or icing of your choice (see recipes right)

1   Preheat the oven to 160°C (315°F/Gas 2–3). Line two baking trays with non-stick baking paper.

2   Use an electric mixer to beat the butter and sugar until pale and creamy. Add the egg and vanilla and beat until combined. Sift the flours together into a bowl, then use a wooden spoon to gently mix in the flours to form a soft dough.

3   Divide the dough into two portions and shape each into a disc. Roll out one portion between two sheets of non-stick baking paper until 5 mm (¼ inch) thick. Use 5 cm (2 inch) cutters to cut out the biscuits and place on the baking trays. Repeat with the remaining dough.

4   Bake in batches for 10–15 minutes or until lightly golden and cooked through. Remove from the oven and leave to cool slightly on the baking trays, then transfer to a wire rack to cool completely.

5   Either sandwich the biscuits together with a filling, or spread with the icing.

FILLINGS AND ICING

Caramel filling: Melt 30 g (1 oz) butter, 100 g (3½ oz/½ cup, lightly packed) light brown sugar and 160 g (5¾ oz/½ cup) condensed milk in a saucepan. Stir over medium heat until the sugar dissolves. Bring to the boil and simmer for 1 minute or until the mixture thickens slightly. Allow to cool, then spread between the biscuits. The filled biscuits will keep for 3–4 days in an airtight container.

Peppermint filling: Combine 250 g (9 oz/2 cups) sifted pure icing (confectioners') sugar, 5–6 teaspoons hot water and a few drops of natural peppermint extract until smooth. Spread between the cooled biscuits. The filled biscuits will keep for 5 days in an airtight container.

Lime butter filling: Beat 60 g (2¼ oz) softened butter and 125 g (4½ oz/1 cup) sifted pure icing (confectioners') sugar until smooth. Beat in the finely shredded zest of 1 lime and 1–2 teaspoons lime juice. Spread between the cooled biscuits. The filled biscuits will keep for 5 days in an airtight container.

Vanilla icing (frosting): Combine 150 g (5½ oz/1¼ cups) sifted pure icing (confectioners') sugar, 1 tablespoon softened butter, ½ teaspoon natural vanilla extract and 2 tablespoons boiling water. Spread over the cooled biscuits. The iced biscuits will keep for 5 days in an airtight container.

> **TIP** Keep un-iced, unfilled biscuits in an airtight container in a cool place for up to 1 week, or freeze in an airtight container for up to 3 months.

Anzac biscuits

A great way to satisfy the troops, both past and present, these biscuits were designed to withstand the long journey to Australian and New Zealand soldiers who were stationed overseas in World War I. This durability, coupled with their slightly chewy texture and caramel taste, makes them a lunchbox favourite.

MAKES about 24   **PREPARATION TIME** 20 minutes   **COOKING TIME** 20 minutes

150 g (5½ oz/1 cup) plain
  (all-purpose) flour
165 g (5¾ oz/¾ cup) caster
  (superfine) sugar
100 g (3½ oz/1 cup) rolled
  (porridge) oats
90 g (3¼ oz/1 cup) desiccated
  coconut
125 g (4½ oz) unsalted butter
90 g (3¼ oz/¼ cup) golden syrup
  (light treacle)
½ teaspoon bicarbonate of soda
  (baking soda)
1 tablespoon boiling water

1   Preheat the oven to 180°C (350°F/ Gas 4). Line two large baking trays with non-stick baking paper.

2   Sift the flour into a large bowl. Stir in the sugar, oats and coconut, then make a well in the centre *(pic 1)*.

3   Combine the butter and golden syrup in a small saucepan. Stir over low heat until the butter has melted and the mixture is smooth. Remove from the heat. Dissolve the bicarbonate of soda in the boiling water and immediately add to the butter mixture, which will foam up instantly *(pic 2)*. Add to the dry ingredients and use a wooden spoon to stir until well combined.

4   Roll level tablespoons of mixture into balls and place on the prepared trays, leaving about 5 cm (2 inches) between each to allow for spreading. Flatten slightly with the base of a glass *(pic 3)*.

5   Bake for 20 minutes or until golden. Leave on the trays for 5 minutes before transferring to a wire rack to cool.

1

2

3

TIP Keep in an airtight container for up to 2 weeks.

Greek almond crescents

Rich and buttery, with flavourings of almond and cinnamon, these biscuits are traditionally made as crescents, but you can roll the dough into balls and flatten slightly before cooking if you prefer.

MAKES about 38 **PREPARATION TIME** 20 minutes **COOKING TIME** 20 minutes

200 g (7 oz) butter, softened slightly
125 g (4½ oz/1 cup) icing
    (confectioners') sugar, sifted,
    plus extra, to dust
1 teaspoon finely grated orange zest
1 egg, at room temperature
1 egg yolk
1 tablespoon brandy
375 g (13 oz/2½ cups) plain
    (all-purpose) flour
1½ teaspoons baking powder
1 teaspoon ground cinnamon
155 g (5½ oz/1 cup) blanched
    almonds, toasted (see tip) and
    finely chopped

1   Preheat the oven to 160°C (315°F/ Gas 2–3).

2   Line two large baking trays with non-stick baking paper.

3   Use an electric mixer to beat the butter, sugar and orange zest in a small bowl until pale and creamy. Add the egg, egg yolk and brandy and continue to beat until well combined.

4   Transfer the mixture to a large bowl. Sift the flour, baking powder and cinnamon together, then stir in the almonds. Add to the butter mixture and use a wooden spoon to mix until well combined *(pic 1)*.

5   Shape level tablespoons of mixture into crescents and place on the trays, leaving about 3 cm (1¼ inches) between each to allow for spreading *(pic 2)*.

6   Bake for 15–20 minutes, swapping the trays around after 10 minutes, or until lightly golden and cooked through. Leave on the trays for 5 minutes before transferring to a wire rack. Dust heavily with icing sugar while still warm *(pic 3)*, then cool to room temperature.

TIPS To toast almonds, spread on a baking tray and cook in a 180°C (350°F/Gas 4) oven for 8 minutes or until pale golden. Cool on tray.
   Dust the biscuits with icing sugar again before serving to freshen them up.
   Keep in an airtight container for up to 1 week.

Viennese fingers

These biscuits are basically a deliciously rich shortbread with the mixture being soft enough to pipe into fingers. Dipping them in chocolate makes them even more tempting.

MAKES about 20   **PREPARATION TIME** 20 minutes (+ cooling and 1 hour setting)   **COOKING TIME** 12 minutes

100 g (3½ oz) unsalted butter,
    softened, plus 30 g (1 oz) extra
40 g (1½ oz/⅓ cup) icing
    (confectioners') sugar
2 egg yolks
1½ teaspoons natural vanilla extract
150 g (5½ oz/1 cup) plain
    (all-purpose) flour
100 g (3½ oz) dark chocolate,
    finely chopped

1 Preheat the oven to 180°C (350°F/ Gas 4). Line two baking trays with non-stick baking paper.

2 Use an electric mixer to beat the butter and icing sugar in a small bowl until pale and creamy. Gradually add the egg yolks and vanilla and beat thoroughly. Transfer to a large bowl, then sift in the flour. Use a flat-bladed knife to mix using a cutting action until the ingredients are just combined and the mixture is smooth.

3 Spoon the mixture into a piping (icing) bag fitted with a 1 cm (½ inch) fluted nozzle (see tip). Pipe the mixture into wavy 8 cm (3¼ inch) lengths on the trays. Bake for 12 minutes, swapping the trays around halfway through cooking, or until light golden brown and cooked through. Cool slightly on the trays before transferring to a wire rack to cool completely.

4 Line one of the trays with a new piece of non-stick baking paper. Place the chocolate and extra butter in a small heatproof bowl. Half-fill a small saucepan with water and bring to the boil, then remove from the heat. Sit the bowl over the pan (make sure the water doesn't touch the base of the bowl). Stir occasionally until the chocolate and butter have melted and the mixture is smooth. Dip half of each biscuit in the chocolate mixture to coat and then place on the lined tray. Set aside for 1 hour or until the chocolate sets.

TIPS To make piping easier, fold down the bag by about 10 cm (4 inches) before spooning the mixture in, then unfold. The top will be clean and easy to twist, stopping the mixture from squirting out.
    Keep in an airtight container for up to 4 days.

Monte creams

These biscuits are reminiscent of a well-known commercially made biscuit, but with that special homemade quality. You can experiment with the icing and jam used to fill them — any of the buttercreams on page 14 will work and use your favourite jam to create your own flavour combinations.

MAKES about 18   **PREPARATION TIME** 20 minutes (+ cooling)   **COOKING TIME** 18 minutes

125 g (4½ oz) unsalted butter, softened
110 g (3¾ oz/½ cup) caster (superfine) sugar
60 ml (2 fl oz/¼ cup) milk
225 g (8 oz/1½ cups) self-raising flour
35 g (1¼ oz/¼ cup) custard powder (instant vanilla pudding mix), plus extra, for dipping
30 g (1 oz/⅓ cup) desiccated coconut

FILLING
50 g (1¾ oz) unsalted butter, softened
60 g (2¼ oz/½ cup) icing (confectioners') sugar, sifted
2 teaspoons milk
115 g (4 oz/⅓ cup) raspberry jam

1 Preheat the oven to 180°C (350°F/ Gas 4). Line two large baking trays with non-stick baking paper.

2 Use an electric mixer to beat the butter and sugar in a medium bowl until pale and creamy. Add the milk and beat until combined.

3 Sift the flour and custard powder together, add to the butter mixture with the coconut *(pic 1)* and use a wooden spoon to mix to a soft dough.

4 Roll 2 teaspoons of mixture into a ball and place on a prepared tray. Repeat with the remaining mixture, leaving about 5 cm (2 inches) between each ball to allow for spreading. Dip a fork in the extra custard powder, then tap off any excess and use to flatten the balls to about 5 cm (2 inch) rounds *(pic 2)*. (You'll need to dip the fork in the custard powder occasionally to prevent it sticking to the dough.)

5 Bake the biscuits for 18 minutes, swapping the trays around halfway through cooking, or until lightly golden. Leave on the trays to cool.

6 Meanwhile, to make the filling, use an electric mixer to beat the butter and icing sugar in a small bowl until pale and creamy. Add the milk and beat until combined. Spread a biscuit with a heaped teaspoon of the icing and spread another biscuit with a teaspoon of jam, then sandwich them together *(pic 3)*. Repeat with the remaining biscuits, icing and jam.

TIP Keep in an airtight container in a cool place (but not in the refrigerator) for up to 2 days.

Almond biscotti

The word biscotti translates from Italian as 'twice-baked', and that's what gives these biscuits their characteristic crunch and makes them ideal for dunking in a hot drink. They've come a long way since their days as a long-life food for Roman soldiers and are now regular fixtures at cafes and restaurants.

MAKES about 60 **PREPARATION TIME** 20 minutes (+ 45 minutes cooling) **COOKING TIME** 45 minutes

250 g (9 oz/1²/₃ cups) plain
(all-purpose) flour
¼ teaspoon bicarbonate of soda
(baking soda)
2 eggs, at room temperature
220 g (7¾ oz/1 cup) caster
(superfine) sugar
1 teaspoon natural vanilla extract
200 g (7 oz) blanched almonds

1   Preheat the oven to 180°C (350°F/ Gas 4). Line two large baking trays with non-stick baking paper.

2   Sift the flour and bicarbonate of soda together. Use an electric mixer to beat the eggs, sugar and vanilla on medium speed for 5–6 minutes or until thick and pale. Add the flour mixture and beat on low speed until just combined and a soft dough forms. Use a wooden spoon to stir in the almonds.

3   Turn the dough out onto a lightly floured work surface and divide into four equal portions. Use lightly floured hands to shape each portion into a log about 12 cm (4½ inches) long *(pic 1)*.

4   Transfer the logs to the lined baking trays, leaving about 7 cm (2¾ inches) between each. Use your hands to flatten the logs slightly so they are about 8 cm (3¼ inches) wide *(pic 2)*.

5   Bake for 25 minutes, swapping the trays around halfway through cooking, or until the logs are light golden and firm to touch. Leave on the trays for 45 minutes to cool.

6   Reduce the oven temperature to 130°C (250°F/Gas 1). Put the logs on a chopping board and use a sharp serrated knife to cut them diagonally into 8 mm (⅜ inch) thick slices *(pic 3)*. Return to the lined trays and bake for 20 minutes, swapping the trays around halfway through cooking, or until light golden. Leave on the trays for 5 minutes, before transferring to a wire rack to cool completely.

VARIATIONS

Pistachio and dried cranberry biscotti: Replace the almonds with 100 g (3½ oz/ ¾ cup) pistachios and 100 g (3½ oz) dried sweetened cranberries.

Coffee and hazelnut biscotti: Replace the vanilla with 2 teaspoons instant coffee granules combined with 1½ teaspoons boiling water (cool before adding). Replace the almonds with 200 g (7 oz) hazelnuts, roasted at 180°C (350°F/Gas 4) for 10 minutes and rubbed with a tea towel (dish towel) while hot to remove the skins (cool before adding).

1

2

3

TIPS It is best to avoid using dark or non-stick baking trays for this recipe as they will add too much colour to the biscotti.
Keep in an airtight container for up to 3 weeks.

Amaretti

Amaretti are light, crisp Italian biscuits, similar to the macaroon, with an almond flavour. They are an especially good biscuit to accompany coffee but can also be crushed and used as a flavoursome filling for baked fruits – make the crushed biscuits into a paste with sugar and butter then stuff into the cored apples or spoon onto the peaches. Then bake the fruit with a little wine added to the ovenproof dish, which adds to the flavour.

MAKES about 40   **PREPARATION TIME** 20 minutes (+ 1 hour standing)   **COOKING TIME** 15–20 minutes

1 tablespoon plain (all-purpose)
   flour
1 tablespoon cornflour (cornstarch)
1 teaspoon ground cinnamon
160 g (5¾ oz/⅔ cup) caster
   (superfine) sugar
1 teaspoon finely grated lemon zest
95 g (3¼ oz/1 cup) ground almonds
2 egg whites
30 g (1 oz/¼ cup) icing
   (confectioners') sugar

1   Line two baking trays with non-stick baking paper. Sift the flour, cornflour, cinnamon and half the caster sugar together into a large bowl, then add the lemon zest and ground almonds.

2   Use an electric mixer with a whisk attachment to whisk the egg whites in a clean, dry bowl until firm peaks form. Gradually add the remaining caster sugar, whisking constantly until the mixture is thick and glossy and all the sugar has dissolved. Use a large metal spoon to fold the dry ingredients into the egg white mixture until just combined.

3   Roll 2 level teaspoons of mixture at a time with oiled or wetted hands into balls and arrange on the trays, allowing room for spreading. Set the trays aside, uncovered, at room temperature for 1 hour.

4   Preheat the oven to 180°C (350°F/ Gas 4). Sift the icing sugar liberally over the biscuits, then bake for 15–20 minutes or until crisp and lightly browned. Transfer to a wire rack and leave to cool completely.

TIP Keep in an airtight container for up to 1 week.

Gingerbread people

This recipe is a great one to involve kids in — they can tint the icing different colours and use their imaginations to 'dress' their little people. They can even add small lollies for decorations.

MAKES about 10   **PREPARATION TIME** 40 minutes (+ 2 hours chilling/cooling/setting)   **COOKING TIME** 12 minutes

125 g (4½ oz) unsalted butter, softened slightly
75 g (2¾ oz/⅓ cup, firmly packed) dark brown or light brown sugar
115 g (4 oz/⅓ cup) golden syrup (light treacle)
1 egg, at room temperature, lightly whisked
375 g (13 oz/2½ cups) plain (all-purpose) flour
50 g (1¾ oz/⅓ cup) self-raising flour
1 tablespoon ground ginger
1 teaspoon bicarbonate of soda (baking soda)

ICING
1 egg white, at room temperature
½ teaspoon lemon juice
125 g (4½ oz/1 cup) pure icing (confectioners') sugar, sifted
Assorted food colourings of your choice

1 Preheat the oven to 180°C (350°F/ Gas 4). Line two large baking trays with non-stick baking paper.

2 Use an electric mixer to beat the butter, sugar and golden syrup in a medium bowl until pale and creamy. Add the egg and beat well.

3 Sift the flours, ginger and bicarbonate of soda together over the butter mixture and use a flat-bladed knife to mix until just combined. Use a well-floured hand to combine the dough thoroughly. Turn onto a floured work surface and knead lightly for 1 minute or until smooth.

4 Divide the dough into two portions and shape each into a disc. Wrap each disc in plastic wrap and refrigerate for 20–30 minutes or until the dough has firmed slightly.

5 Evenly roll out one disc between two sheets of non-stick baking paper to a thickness of 5 mm (¼ inch) (pic 1). Transfer to a tray and repeat with remaining disc. Refrigerate for 15 minutes or until firm enough to cut.

6 Use gingerbread people cutters to cut the dough into shapes (pic 2) and place on the lined trays, leaving about 3 cm (1¼ inches) between each to allow for spreading. Re-roll and cut out any scraps. Bake for 12 minutes or until the biscuits are lightly browned and cooked through. Cool completely on the trays.

7 To make the icing (frosting), put the egg white in a small dry bowl. Use an electric mixer with a whisk attachment to whisk the egg white until foamy. Add the lemon juice and then gradually whisk in the icing sugar, whisking well after each addition, until thick and creamy. Divide the icing among bowls, depending on how many colours you want. Tint each bowl of icing with food colouring. Spoon into small paper piping (icing) bags or snap-lock bags and seal the open ends. Snip the tips off the bags, then pipe faces and clothing onto the cooled biscuits (pic 3). Set aside for 1 hour or until the icing sets.

TIP Keep in an airtight container for up to 1 week.

Scottish shortbread

MAKES 16 pieces   **PREPARATION TIME** 15 minutes (+ 20 minutes chilling)   **COOKING TIME** 35 minutes

250 g (9 oz) butter, softened slightly
110 g (3¾ oz/½ cup) caster
  (superfine) sugar
335 g (11¾ oz/2¼ cups) plain
  (all-purpose) flour
45 g (1¾ oz/¼ cup) rice flour
1 tablespoon sugar, to sprinkle

1   Preheat the oven to 160°C (315°F/
Gas 2–3). Trace around a round
20 cm (8 inch) cake tin to mark a
circle on each of two sheets of non-
stick baking paper *(pic 1)*, then turn
them over.

2   Use an electric mixer to beat
the butter and sugar until pale and
creamy. Sift the flours together.
Add to the butter mixture and use
a flat-bladed knife to mix to a soft
dough. Gather together with your
fingertips, then divide into two
equal portions. Shape each portion
into a disc and wrap in plastic wrap.
Refrigerate for 20 minutes.

3   Use a lightly floured rolling pin
to roll out a portion of dough on each
sheet of baking paper to fit the marked
circles. Neaten the edges, then use
your thumb and index finger to pinch
to create a decorative edge *(pic 2)*.
Place each round, still on the baking
paper, on a baking tray. Use a sharp
knife to mark each round into eight
wedges. Prick the surface with a fork
(pic 3) and sprinkle with sugar.

4   Bake the shortbread for
35 minutes, swapping the trays around
halfway through cooking, or until
pale golden and cooked through.
Leave on the trays to cool. Cut into
wedges to serve.

VARIATION

Shortbread fingers: Roll the dough
out between two sheets of non-stick
baking paper to a rectangle 1 cm
(½ inch) thick. Use a ruler as a guide
to cut the dough into 2 x 7 cm
(¾ x 2¾ inch) fingers. Place on baking
trays lined with non-stick baking
paper, leaving about 2 cm (¾ inch)
between each. Prick the surface of
each biscuit with a fork and sprinkle
with the sugar. Bake for 20–25
minutes or until lightly golden and
cooked through. Leave on the trays for
5 minutes then transfer to a wire rack
to cool.

3

2

1

TIP Keep in an airtight
container for up to 1 week.

Langues de chat

Langues de chat translates from French as cats' tongues, referring to the biscuit's shape. They are often served with ice creams, sorbets, and other iced or soft desserts such as mousse and sabayon. These delicious sponge-like biscuits are also perfect served along side tea and coffee.

MAKES 24   **PREPARATION TIME** 25 minutes   **COOKING TIME** 6–8 minutes

75 g (2¾ oz) unsalted butter, softened
90 g (3¼ oz/⅓ cup) caster (superfine) sugar
2 egg whites
75 g (2¾ oz/½ cup) plain (all-purpose) flour, sifted
Icing (confectioners') sugar, to dust

1   Preheat the oven to 220°C (425°F/ Gas 7). Line two baking trays with non-stick baking paper (see tip).

2   Use an electric mixer to beat the butter and caster sugar in a small bowl until pale and creamy. Whisk the egg whites in a small bowl with a fork until frothy, then gradually add to the butter mixture, beating well after each addition. Use a large metal spoon or spatula to lightly fold in the sifted flour and a pinch of salt until well combined.

3   Spoon the mixture into a piping bag fitted with a 1 cm (½ inch) plain nozzle and pipe 12 biscuits, 8cm (3¼ inches) long, onto each tray. Bake for 6–8 minutes, swapping the trays halfway through cooking, or until cooked through and golden around the edges. Cool on the trays for 2 minutes, then transfer to a wire rack to cool completely. Dust with icing sugar just before serving.

TIPS   They can also be piped into and cooked in lightly buttered langues de chat tins (as we have done), available from selected kitchenware stores.
Keep in an airtight container for up to 2 days.

Digestive biscuits

Also known as wheatmeal biscuits, these are made with a pastry-like dough using wholemeal flour and unprocessed bran. Despite their name, they do not have any special 'digestive' properties. They can be eaten plain, served with blue cheese and honey, or spread or drizzled with melted chocolate.

MAKES about 25   **PREPARATION TIME** 35 minutes (+ 1 hour 20 minutes chilling)   **COOKING TIME** 15 minutes

125 g (4½ oz) butter, softened
60 g (2¼ oz/⅓ cup, lightly packed) light brown sugar
1 tablespoon malt extract
1 egg, at room temperature, lightly whisked
150 g (5½ oz/1 cup) plain (all-purpose) flour
150 g (5½ oz/1 cup) plain (all-purpose) wholemeal (whole-wheat) flour
1 teaspoon baking powder
35 g (1¼ oz/½ cup) unprocessed bran

1   Use an electric mixer to beat the butter, sugar and malt extract in a medium bowl until pale and creamy. Add the egg and beat well.

2   Sift the flours and baking powder together into a bowl, returning the husks to the bowl (*pic 1*). Add to the butter mixture with the bran and use a wooden spoon and then your hands to mix until evenly combined and a dough forms. Gather together and shape into a disc, then wrap in plastic wrap and refrigerate for 1 hour or until firm enough to roll.

3   Preheat the oven to 180°C (350°F/ Gas 4). Line two baking trays with non-stick baking paper.

4   Roll out half the dough between two sheets of baking paper to 4 mm (¼ inch) thick (*pic 2*). Use a 7 cm (2¾ inch) cutter to cut out the biscuits and place them on the lined trays (*pic 3*). Prick the surface of each once with a fork. Repeat with the remaining dough, re-rolling any scraps. Refrigerate for 20 minutes to firm.

5   Bake the biscuits for 15 minutes, swapping the trays around halfway through cooking, or until golden brown and cooked through. Leave on the trays for 5 minutes then transfer to a wire rack to cool completely.

TIP Keep in an airtight container for up to 2 weeks.

Florentines

Although their name sounds Italian in origin, Austrian bakers are the ones credited with creating this heavenly combination of nuts, dried fruit, honey, butter and spice, finished with a chocolate coating. They're chewy and more-ish, and can be made any size you like (simply adjust the cooking time to suit).

MAKES about 25   **PREPARATION TIME** 20 minutes (+ cooling and setting)   **COOKING TIME** 20 minutes

190 g (6¾ oz/2 cups) flaked
   almonds
260 g (9¼ oz) dried sweetened
   cranberries or glacé cherries
150 g (5½ oz/1 cup) mixed peel
   (mixed candied citrus peel)
75 g (2¾ oz/½ cup) plain
   (all-purpose) flour, sifted
½ teaspoon ground nutmeg
Finely grated zest of 1 orange
260 g (9¼ oz/¾ cup) honey
165 g (5¾ oz/¾ cup) caster
   (superfine) sugar
30 g (1 oz) unsalted butter, chopped
330 g (11½ oz) dark couverture
   chocolate (70% cocoa solids),
   finely chopped

1 Preheat the oven to 190°C (375°F/ Gas 5). Line two large baking trays with non-stick baking paper.

2 Put the flaked almonds, dried cranberries, mixed peel, flour, nutmeg and orange zest in a large bowl and mix to combine.

3 Put the honey, sugar and butter in a small saucepan over low heat and stir occasionally until melted and combined. Increase the heat to medium and simmer until the mixture reaches 115°C (239°F) on a sugar thermometer (*pic 1*). Pour over the dry ingredients and use a wooden spoon to mix until well combined.

4 Place heaped tablespoons of the mixture on the lined trays, leaving about 7 cm (2¾ inches) between each. (You will need to bake the biscuits in two batches.) Use the back of a teaspoon, dipped in hot water as often as needed to prevent sticking, to flatten each ball into a round about 7.5 cm (3 inches) in diameter (*pic 2*). Bake for 8–10 minutes or until the almonds are golden and the mixture has bubbled slightly. Cool completely on the trays.

5 Put the chocolate in a heatproof bowl over a saucepan of simmering water (make sure the base of the bowl doesn't touch the water). Stir occasionally until melted and smooth. Set aside to cool slightly. Turn the florentines over so the flat side is facing up and spread 2 teaspoons of melted chocolate over each. Set aside to firm a little, then use a fork to make a wavy pattern in the chocolate, if desired (*pic 3*). Place in the refrigerator to set.

1

2

3

TIP Keep in airtight containers, layered with non-stick baking paper, in the refrigerator for up to 1 week. Stand at room temperature for 15 minutes before serving.

Crackle cookies

Coating these biscuits with icing sugar before cooking results in a very effective 'crackle' pattern. Studded with pecans, they are truly addictive.

MAKES about 50   **PREPARATION TIME** 25 minutes (+ 3 hours or overnight chilling)   **COOKING TIME** 20–25 minutes

125 g (4½ oz) unsalted butter, softened
370 g (13 oz/2 cups, lightly packed) light brown sugar
2 eggs
1 teaspoon natural vanilla extract
60 g (2¼ oz) good-quality dark chocolate, chopped, melted and cooled
80 ml (2½ fl oz/⅓ cup) milk
410 g (14½ oz/2¾ cups) plain (all-purpose) flour
2 tablespoons unsweetened cocoa powder
2 teaspoons baking powder
¼ teaspoon ground allspice
85 g (3 oz/⅔ cup) chopped pecans
Icing (confectioners') sugar, to dust

1   Use an electric mixer to beat the butter and sugar until well combined. Add the eggs, one at a time, beating well after each addition. Stir in the vanilla, chocolate and milk.

2   Sift the flour, cocoa, baking powder, allspice and a pinch of salt together into the butter mixture and use a wooden spoon to mix well. Stir in the pecans, then refrigerate for at least 3 hours or overnight until the mixture is firm.

3   Preheat the oven to 180°C (350°F/ Gas 4). Line a large baking tray with non-stick baking paper.

4   Sift the icing sugar onto a plate. Roll tablespoonfuls of the cookie mixture into balls, then roll each one in the icing sugar to coat well. Place on the baking trays, spacing them well apart to allow for spreading.

5   Bake for 20–25 minutes or until just firm. Remove from the oven and leave to cool on the trays for 3–4 minutes, then transfer to a wire rack to cool completely.

> **TIP** Keep in an airtight container for up to 1 week, or freeze for up to 3 months.

Melting moments

These enormously popular biscuits have a sublime melt-in-the-mouth texture teamed with a smooth buttercream filling. Experiment with different flavoured buttercreams to suit your tastes. You can make regular shaped biscuits by using a plain nozzle in the piping bag.

MAKES about 20   **PREPARATION TIME** 30 minutes (+ cooling)   **COOKING TIME** 12 minutes

150 g (5½ oz/1 cup) plain (all-purpose) flour
40 g (1½ oz/⅓ cup) cornflour (cornstarch)
180 g (6¼ oz) unsalted butter, softened slightly
40 g (1½ oz/⅓ cup) icing (confectioners') sugar
1 teaspoon natural vanilla extract
1 quantity citrus buttercream

1 Preheat the oven to 180°C (350°F/Gas 4). Line two large baking trays with non-stick baking paper.

2 Sift the flours together. Use an electric mixer to beat the butter, icing sugar and vanilla in a medium bowl until pale and creamy. Add the sifted flours and beat on low speed until just combined, scraping down the side of the bowl when necessary.

3 Spoon the mixture into a piping (icing) bag fitted with a 1 cm (½ inch) fluted nozzle. Hold the nozzle 1 cm (½ inch) above a lined tray and pipe the mixture in rosettes, 4 cm (1½ inches) in diameter, leaving about 5 cm (2 inches) between each *(pic 1)*.

4 Bake the biscuits for 12 minutes, swapping the trays around halfway through cooking, or until pale golden and cooked through. Leave on the trays for 5 minutes before transferring to a wire rack to cool *(pic 2)*.

5 Spread a cooled biscuit with the citrus buttercream and then sandwich with another biscuit *(pic 3)*. Repeat with the remaining biscuits and buttercream.

1

2

3

TIP Keep in an airtight container in a cool place, but not the refrigerator, for up to 3 days.

Tuiles

The curved shape of these delicate biscuits was thought to resemble a tile (tuile in French). For perfect tuiles, you need to ensure the mixture is spread into rounds of even thickness, and the biscuits must be removed from the trays and shaped quickly. For this reason, it's wise to cook only a few at a time.

MAKES 20–25   **PREPARATION TIME** 25 minutes (+ 1 hour chilling)   **COOKING TIME** 7–8 minutes per batch

110 g (3¾ oz) butter
125 g (4½ oz/1 cup) icing
  (confectioners') sugar, sifted
3 egg whites, at room temperature
110 g (3¾ oz/¾ cup) plain
  (all-purpose) flour, sifted
½ teaspoon natural vanilla extract
Nuts (such as flaked almonds or
  finely chopped pecans, walnuts
  or macadamias) and/or finely
  chopped dark chocolate (optional)

1   Heat the butter in a small saucepan over low heat until just melted. Remove from the heat and set aside for 5 minutes to cool slightly.

2   Put the icing sugar in a food processor. Add the egg whites and process until well combined. Add the flour and vanilla and process briefly, until smooth (*pic 1*). Add the melted butter and pulse until just combined. Transfer to a small bowl, cover and refrigerate for 1 hour or until chilled.

3   Preheat the oven to 170°C (325°F/ Gas 3). Line a baking tray with non-stick baking paper or a silpat mat.

4   Use a small palette knife to spread teaspoons of the mixture into four 9 cm (3½ inch) diameter circles or 5 x 12 cm (2 x 4½ inch) rectangles/ ovals using the back of a teaspoon (*pic 2*). They need to be quite thin and even or the end product won't be crisp. Lightly sprinkle with nuts and/ or chocolate, if desired.

5   Bake the tuiles, in batches, for 7–8 minutes or until golden. Have two rolling pins ready. Immediately use a palette knife to transfer the tuiles to the rolling pins and set aside to cool (*pic 3*). Repeat with the remaining mixture.

1

2

3

TIPS The uncooked mixture will keep, covered, in the refrigerator for up to 1 week so you can make tuiles as you need them.
   Keep cooked biscuits in an airtight container for up to 3 days.

Parmesan biscuits

There are many versions of cheese biscuits and these ones are crisp and buttery with a piquant flavour courtesy of the parmesan cheese. They make an excellent accompaniment to a glass of wine and are also a popular choice for a gift.

MAKES about 26   **PREPARATION TIME** 20 minutes   **COOKING TIME** 12 minutes

150 g (5½ oz) unsalted butter, softened
100 g (3½ oz/1 cup) finely grated parmesan cheese
35 g (1¼ oz/⅓ cup, loosely packed) finely shredded cheddar cheese
185 g (6½ oz/1¼ cups) plain (all-purpose) flour
25 g (1 oz/¼ cup) finely grated parmesan cheese, extra
½ teaspoon sweet paprika (optional)
2 teaspoons sesame seeds (optional)

1   Preheat the oven to 180°C (350°F/ Gas 4). Line two large baking trays with non-stick baking paper.

2   Use an electric mixer to beat the butter in a medium bowl until pale and creamy. Add the cheeses and beat until combined. Add the flour and use a flat-bladed knife in a cutting action to mix to a rough dough (*pic 1*). Turn out onto a lightly floured work surface and press together until smooth.

3   Use a rolling pin to roll the dough between two sheets of non-stick baking paper to 5 mm (¼ inch) thick (*pic 2*). Use a lightly floured 4 cm (1½ inch) round cutter to cut out biscuits and place them on the prepared trays, leaving about 5 cm (2 inches) between each to allow for spreading. Re-roll and cut any remaining dough. Sprinkle with the extra parmesan combined with a little paprika and/or sesame seeds (*pic 3*), if desired.

4   Bake the biscuits for 12 minutes, swapping the trays around halfway through cooking, or until golden and cooked through. Leave on the trays to cool completely.

1

2

3

TIP Keep in an airtight container for up to 1 week.

Vanilla meringues

MAKES about 14   **PREPARATION TIME** 15 minutes   **COOKING TIME** 1 hour 10 minutes

2 egg whites (see tip)
1 vanilla bean, split lengthways and
   seeds scraped (see tip)
110 g (3¾ oz/½ cup) caster
   (superfine) sugar
1 teaspoon cornflour (cornstarch)

1   Preheat the oven to 120°C (235°F/ Gas ½). Line two baking trays with non-stick baking paper.

2   Put the egg whites and vanilla seeds in a clean, dry medium bowl. Use an electric mixer with a whisk attachment to whisk on medium speed until soft peaks form. Gradually add the sugar, 1 tablespoon at a time *(pic 1)*, whisking well after each addition. Continue whisking until the sugar has dissolved and the meringue is thick and glossy. Whisk in the cornflour.

3   Drop heaped tablespoons of the meringue onto the prepared trays, leaving about 3 cm (1¼ inches) between each *(pic 2)*. Reduce the oven temperature to 100°C (200°F/ Gas ½) and bake the meringues for 1 hour 10 minutes or until they are crisp and sound hollow when tapped *(pic 3)*. Turn off the oven and leave the meringues to cool in the oven with the door ajar.

VARIATIONS

Rosewater and pistachio meringues:
Omit the vanilla bean. Whisk 3 teaspoons rosewater into the meringue mixture after the sugar. Sprinkle the meringues with 2 tablespoons finely chopped unsalted pistachio nuts before baking.

Orange and almond meringues: Omit the vanilla bean. Beat in 1 teaspoon finely grated orange zest with the sugar. Fold 2 tablespoons toasted slivered almonds into the meringue mixture after whisking in the sugar. Sprinkle the meringues with 2 tablespoons slivered almonds before baking.

1

2

3

TIPS   To ensure egg whites whisk to their greatest potential volume, use eggs that are at room temperature and a clean, dry mixing bowl.
   You can replace the vanilla bean seeds with 1 teaspoon natural vanilla extract or ½ teaspoon vanilla bean paste if you prefer.
   Keep in an airtight container for up to 1 week.

Espresso meringue kisses

Light and crisp coffee-flavoured meringues with a delectable chocolate ganache filling, these sweet treats are perfect little bites to have with an afternoon coffee or to serve guests after dinner.

MAKES 28   **PREPARATION TIME** 20 minutes (+ cooling and 30 minutes chilling)   **COOKING TIME** 30 minutes

2 teaspoons instant coffee granules
1 tablespoon boiling water
2 egg whites, at room temperature
110 g (3¾ oz/½ cup) caster
  (superfine) sugar
2 teaspoons cornflour (cornstarch)

CHOCOLATE GANACHE
100 g (3½ oz) dark chocolate,
  chopped
60 ml (2 fl oz/¼ cup) pouring
  (whipping) cream

1 Preheat the oven to 150°C (300°F/ Gas 2). Brush two large baking trays with melted butter or oil, then line with non-stick baking paper.

2 Dissolve the coffee in the boiling water and set aside to cool.

3 Put the egg whites in a clean, dry medium bowl. Use an electric mixer with a whisk attachment to whisk on medium speed until soft peaks form. Gradually add the sugar, 1 tablespoon at a time, whisking well after each addition. Continue whisking until the sugar has dissolved and the meringue is thick and glossy. Whisk in the cornflour and cooled coffee mixture until just combined (pic 1).

4 Spoon the meringue into a piping (icing) bag fitted with a 1 cm (½ inch) plain nozzle. Holding the nozzle about 1 cm above the lined trays, pipe small swirls to make 2 cm (¾ inch) meringues, leaving about 3 cm (1¼ inches) between each (pic 2).

5 Bake the meringues for 30 minutes, swapping the trays around halfway through cooking, or until dry to touch. Turn off the oven and leave the meringues to cool in the oven with the door ajar.

6 Meanwhile, make the chocolate ganache. Put the chocolate and cream in a small saucepan over low heat and stir until the chocolate has melted and the mixture is smooth. Transfer to a small bowl. Refrigerate for 30 minutes, stirring occasionally, or until thickened to a spreadable consistency.

7 Spread the base of a cooled meringue with a little ganache and sandwich with another meringue. Repeat with the remaining meringues and ganache.

1

2

3

TIP Keep in an airtight container in a cool, dry place for up to 3 days.

Macarons

MAKES 24   **PREPARATION TIME** 35 minutes (+ 25 minutes standing, 30 minutes chilling, and cooling)
COOKING TIME 36–45 minutes

125 g (4½ oz/1¼ cups)
   almond meal
215 g (7½ oz/1¾ cups) icing
   (confectioners') sugar
3 egg whites, at room temperature
55 g (2 oz/¼ cup) caster
   (superfine) sugar
1 quantity buttercream (see
   page 14), or ganache filling
   (see below)

1   Grease three large baking trays,
then line with non-stick baking paper.

2   Process the almond meal and
icing sugar in a food processor until
well combined. Put the egg whites
and sugar in a clean, dry medium bowl
and use an electric mixer with a whisk
attachment to whisk on medium speed
until thick and glossy.

3   Sift the almond meal mixture
over the egg whites and use a spatula
or large metal spoon to fold together
until combined. As you continue to
fold, the mixture will start to loosen
up. The texture you need is when it
falls slowly off the spatula *(pic 1)*.

4   Transfer the mixture to a piping
(icing) bag fitted with a 1 cm (½ inch)
plain nozzle. Hold the nozzle about
1 cm above the tray and pipe straight
down to make 4 cm (1½ inch) rounds,
leaving 3 cm (1¼ inches) between each
(pic 2). The macarons should soften
slightly once piped, spreading to about
4.5 cm (1¾ inches). The peak should
also soften, leaving a smooth top.
If not, gently flatten the peak with
a wet finger.

5   Set aside at room temperature
for 25 minutes or until a skin forms.
After 10 minutes, preheat the oven
to 140°C (275°F/Gas 1). Gently touch
a macaron to check a light skin has
formed *(pic 3)* and they are ready
to bake. On humid days this may
take longer.

6   Bake the macarons, one tray at
a time, for 12–15 minutes or until
they have a firm outer shell. Leave on
the tray for 2 minutes, then remove a
macaron and check the base is cooked.
If it is slightly sticky, return them to
the oven for 2–3 minutes and then
check again. Cool completely on
the trays.

7   Match up similar-sized pairs of
macarons. Make the buttercream
(see tip). Transfer to a piping (icing)
bag with a 1 cm (½ inch) plain nozzle,
then pipe onto the base of half the
macarons and top each with its pair.
Chill for 30 minutes. Before serving
the macarons, remove them from
the refrigerator and stand at room
temperature for 10 minutes.

GANACHE FILLING
Stir 100 g (3½ oz) dark chocolate
(70% cocoa solids), chopped, and 125 ml
(4 fl oz/½ cup) pouring (whipping)
cream over low heat until melted
and smooth. Transfer to a bowl and
cool to room temperature, stirring
occasionally. Chill for 20–30 minutes,
stirring occasionally, or until thick
enough to pipe. Use a piping bag with
a 7 mm (⅜ inch) plain nozzle to fill
the macarons with the ganache.

1

2

3

TIPS In warm weather, chill
the buttercream for 15–30
minutes before using.
   To make chocolate
macaron shells, process
1½ tablespoons sifted good-
quality unsweetened cocoa
powder with the icing sugar
and almond meal.
   Keep the filled macarons
in an airtight container in the
refrigerator for up to 4 days.
Serve at room temperature.

Slices

Chocolate caramel slice

A combination of crisp biscuit, sweet caramel and rich dark chocolate make this slice a firm favourite with all ages. It's popular, simple to make and keeps well, so it's a great recipe to add to your baking repertoire. Serve it for morning or afternoon tea or as an indulgent after-dinner treat.

MAKES about 24 pieces **PREPARATION TIME** 15 minutes (+ cooling and setting) **COOKING TIME** 45 minutes

50 g (1¾ oz/⅓ cup) plain
(all-purpose) flour
50 g (1¾ oz/⅓ cup) self-raising
flour
60 g (2¼ oz/⅔ cup) desiccated
coconut
75 g (2¾ oz/⅓ cup, firmly packed)
light brown sugar
65 g (2¼ oz) butter, melted and
cooled

FILLING
2 x 395 g (14 oz) tins condensed milk
115 g (4 oz/⅓ cup) golden syrup
(light treacle)
60 g (2¼ oz) butter, chopped

TOPPING
125 g (4½ oz) dark chocolate,
chopped
30 g (1 oz) butter

1 Preheat the oven to 180°C (350°F/ Gas 4). Line the base and sides of a shallow 18 x 28 cm (7 x 11¼ inch) tin with a piece of non-stick baking paper, cutting into the corners to fit and allowing the paper to extend about 5 cm (2 inches) above the sides.

2 Sift the flours together into a medium mixing bowl. Stir in the coconut and sugar and make a well in the centre. Add the butter and use a wooden spoon to stir until well combined. Use the back of a spoon to press the mixture firmly over the base of the lined tin (*pic 1*). Bake for 12–15 minutes or until lightly coloured. Set aside.

3 To make the filling, combine the condensed milk, golden syrup and butter in a small saucepan. Use a wooden spoon to stir constantly over low heat for about 10 minutes, until the mixture boils and darkens in colour slightly (*pic 2*). Immediately pour over the pastry base. Bake for 15 minutes or until golden brown. Transfer to a wire rack and allow to cool in the tin.

4 To make the topping, combine the chocolate and butter in a heatproof bowl over a saucepan of simmering water (make sure the base of the bowl doesn't touch the water). Stir with a metal spoon until the chocolate has melted and the mixture is smooth. Remove from the heat and cool slightly.

5 Remove the slice from the tin. Spread the topping over the cooled filling (*pic 3*). Set aside at room temperature until the chocolate sets (see tip). Cut into squares or fingers to serve.

2

1

3

> **TIPS** On a warm day you may need to put the slice in the refrigerator to help the chocolate set.
>   Keep in an airtight container, layered with non-stick baking paper, in a cool place for up to 5 days. Refrigerate the slice if the weather is warm.

Brownies

Slightly more cakey than fudgy, this brownie is rich and decadent. Serve it with a cuppa, or warm with ice cream and chocolate sauce for a fuss-free dessert. Good-quality dark chocolate, with 50–70% cocoa solids, will give the best result. Try our variations for a twist on this traditional recipe.

MAKES about 15 pieces   **PREPARATION TIME** 15 minutes   **COOKING TIME** 30–35 minutes

220 g (7¾ oz) dark chocolate, chopped
90 g (3¼ oz) unsalted butter, chopped
4 eggs, at room temperature
165 g (5¾ oz/¾ cup) caster (superfine) sugar
60 g (2¼ oz/¼ cup, firmly packed) light brown sugar
1 teaspoon natural vanilla extract
50 g (1¾ oz/⅓ cup) plain (all-purpose) flour
2 tablespoons unsweetened cocoa powder, plus extra, to dust

1   Preheat the oven to 170°C (325°F/ Gas 3). Brush the base and sides of a shallow 18 x 28 cm (7 x 11¼ inch) tin with melted butter or oil, then line the base and two long sides with a piece of non-stick baking paper, extending over the sides.

2   Put the chocolate and butter in a heatproof bowl over a saucepan of simmering water (make sure the base of the bowl doesn't touch the water). Stir often until melted and smooth *(pic 1)*. Remove from the heat and set aside.

3   Use an electric mixer to beat the eggs, sugars and vanilla for 2 minutes or until pale and starting to thicken. Use a balloon whisk to whisk in the warm chocolate mixture *(pic 2)*. Sift the flour and cocoa together over the top *(pic 3)* and whisk until just combined.

4   Pour the mixture into the prepared tin and smooth the surface with the back of a spoon. Bake for 25–30 minutes or until a skewer inserted into the centre comes out clean. Transfer to a wire rack and allow to cool in the tin.

5   Dust with the extra cocoa and cut into squares or fingers to serve.

VARIATIONS

Raspberry brownies: Spoon half the brownie mixture into the prepared tin and spread evenly. Sprinkle with 100 g (3½ oz) fresh or frozen raspberries, then spoon over the remaining mixture and smooth the top. Dust with icing (confectioners') sugar to serve.

Malt and chocolate chunk brownies: Beat 55 g (2 oz/½ cup) malted milk powder with the eggs, sugars and vanilla. Fold 100 g (3½ oz) good-quality milk chocolate, cut into 1 cm (½ inch) chunks, through the brownie mixture before pouring into the tin. Dust with extra malted milk powder to serve.

TIP Keep in an airtight container, layered with non-stick baking paper, for up to 5 days.

Hazelnut meringue and chocolate fingers

MAKES 24 fingers   **PREPARATION TIME** 30 minutes (+ cooling and 2 hours chilling)   **COOKING TIME** 25 minutes

220 g (7¾ oz/2 cups) hazelnut meal
85 g (3 oz/⅔ cup) icing
   (confectioners') sugar, plus extra,
   to dust
2 tablespoons good-quality
   unsweetened cocoa powder,
   plus extra, to dust
30 g (1 oz/¼ cup) cornflour
   (cornstarch)
6 egg whites, at room temperature
⅛ teaspoon cream of tartar
220 g (7¾ oz/1 cup) caster
   (superfine) sugar

GANACHE
330 g (11½ oz) dark couverture
   chocolate (70% cocoa solids),
   finely chopped
300 ml (10½ fl oz) pouring
   (whipping) cream
75 g (2¾ oz) unsalted butter, diced,
   at room temperature

1   Preheat oven to 130°C (250°F/
Gas 1). Lightly grease three baking
trays. Cut non-stick baking paper to fit
each tray and draw a 24 x 28 cm (9½ x
11¼ inch) rectangle on each, then turn
over and press onto trays. Brush with
melted butter; dust with extra cocoa.

2   Sift hazelnut meal, icing sugar,
cocoa and cornflour into a bowl.

3   Put egg whites and cream of tartar
in a separate clean, dry large bowl
and use an electric mixer with a whisk
attachment to whisk on medium until
foamy. Add sugar, 1 tablespoon at a
time, whisking after each addition.
Continue whisking until sugar has
dissolved and mixture is thick and

glossy. Use a spatula or large metal
spoon to fold in cocoa mixture, in
three batches, until just incorporated.

4   Divide mixture evenly among
marked rectangles and use a palette
knife or spatula to spread it to the edge
of each rectangle *(pic 1)*. Bake for
10 minutes, then rotate and swap trays
around in oven. Bake for 5 minutes
longer or until meringue on top tray
is starting to colour a little at the
edges, but is still soft. Remove top tray
from oven. Bake remaining meringues
for 6 minutes, swapping trays around
after 3 minutes. Cool on trays, then
refrigerate (on trays) to chill.

5   To make ganache, put chocolate
in a heatproof bowl. Bring cream to
the boil over medium heat, pour over
chocolate and stir with a whisk until
smooth. Set aside for 15 minutes,
stirring occasionally, to cool slightly.
Add butter and stir until combined
(pic 2). Set aside at room temperature.

6   Line a large baking tray with non-
stick baking paper. Flip a meringue
layer onto the baking paper. Peel off top
paper *(pic 3)*. Spread half the ganache
over meringue. Repeat to flip another
meringue layer on top and spread
with remaining ganache. Place final
meringue layer on top of ganache (don't
flip over). Put a fresh piece of baking
paper on top and place a baking tray on
it. Gently press to ensure even layers.

7   Chill for 2 hours or until ganache
is set. Trim edges with a knife, then cut
into fingers. Dust with icing sugar.

TIP Keep in an airtight
container, separated by
pieces of non-stick baking
paper, in the refrigerator for
up to 2 days.

Peanut toffee shortbreads

MAKES about 18 pieces   **PREPARATION TIME** 25 minutes (+ 25 minutes cooling)   **COOKING TIME** 20 minutes

110 g (3¾ oz) unsalted butter,
   softened
110 g (3¾ oz/½ cup) caster
   (superfine) sugar
1 egg
225 g (8 oz/1½ cups) plain
   (all-purpose) flour
75 g (2¾ oz/½ cup) self-raising flour

TOPPING
180 g (6 oz) unsalted butter, diced
185 g (6½ oz/1 cup, lightly packed)
   light brown sugar
2 tablespoons golden syrup (light
   treacle) or dark corn syrup
½ teaspoon lemon juice
400 g (14 oz/2½ cups) unsalted
   roasted peanuts

1   Preheat the oven to 180°C (350°F/Gas 4). Lightly grease an 18 x 28 cm (7 x 11¼ inch) tin and line the base and sides with non-stick baking paper, leaving the paper hanging over the two long sides.

2   Use an electric mixer to beat the butter and sugar until pale and creamy. Add the egg and beat well. Sift the flours together into a bowl, then use a wooden spoon to stir into the butter mixture until just combined. Press the mixture evenly over the base of the prepared tin.

3   Bake for 15 minutes or until the shortbread is firm and lightly coloured. Remove from the oven and leave to cool in the tin for 10 minutes.

4   Meanwhile, to make the topping, put the butter, sugar, golden syrup and lemon juice in a saucepan. Stir over low heat until the sugar has dissolved, then simmer, stirring occasionally, for 5 minutes. Stir in the peanuts and remove from the heat.

5   Use two spoons to spread the topping over the shortbread base, taking care as the mixture will be very hot.

6   Bake for a further 5 minutes. Remove from the oven and leave to cool in the tin for 15 minutes, then turn out onto a board and use a large knife to cut into fingers.

TIP Keep in an airtight container in a cool place for up to 1 week, or freeze in an airtight container for up to 1 month. Thaw at room temperature.

Cutting a slice

When cutting a slice always follow the recipe instructions as to whether you should do this while it's warm or when it's cooled. If you remove it from the tin too early, it may break or crumble. Remove the whole slice from the tin to cut it up, and use a ruler as a guide to ensure even squares or fingers.

A long, sharp knife is easier to use and steadier than a small knife. Wipe the knife of crumbs or other mixture in between cuts so that it will cut cleanly and not drag the slice. Diamond shapes are easy: first make parallel cuts lengthways, then cut diagonally across the pan.

Pecan coffee slice

MAKES about 20 pieces   **PREPARATION TIME** 40 minutes   **COOKING TIME** 30 minutes

125 g (4½ oz/1¼ cups) pecans
175 g (6 oz) blanched almonds
2 tablespoons plain (all-purpose)
   flour
165 g (5¾ oz/¾ cup) sugar
7 egg whites
20 chocolate-coated coffee beans,
   to decorate

COFFEE CREAM
200 g (7 oz) unsalted butter,
   softened
150 g (5½ oz) dark chocolate,
   melted and cooled
3–4 teaspoons instant coffee
   granules dissolved in
   2 teaspoons water

1 Preheat the oven to 180°C (350°F/ Gas 4). Lightly grease a shallow 23 cm (9 inch) square tin and line the base and sides with two strips of non-stick baking paper extending over the sides.

2 Toast the pecans and almonds on a baking tray for 5–10 minutes or until golden. Cool slightly, then chop in a food processor until finely ground. Transfer to a bowl. Add the flour and 110 g (3¾ oz/½ cup) of the sugar and mix well.

3 Use an electric mixer with a whisk attachment to whisk the egg whites in a clean, dry large bowl until soft peaks form. Gradually add the remaining sugar, whisking until the mixture is thick and glossy and the sugar has dissolved. Use a large metal spoon or spatula to fold in the nut mixture, a third at a time, until just combined. Spoon into the tin and smooth the surface.

4 Bake for 20 minutes or until springy when touched. Leave in the tin for 5 minutes, then lift out, using the paper as handles, and transfer to a wire rack to cool completely.

5 Meanwhile, to make the coffee cream, use electric beaters to beat the butter in a bowl until pale and creamy. Gradually pour in the melted chocolate and beat well. Add the coffee mixture to the chocolate mixture and mix well. Refrigerate for 5–10 minutes or until slightly thickened.

6 Use a sharp, serrated knife to evenly cut the slice in half horizontally. Carefully remove the top layer and spread half the coffee cream over the base. Replace the top and spread evenly with the remaining cream. Run a palette knife backwards and forwards across the top to create a lined pattern. Place the coffee beans at even intervals on the top. Refrigerate until firm. Trim the edges and cut into squares or fingers. Serve at room temperature.

> **TIP** Keep in an airtight container in the refrigerator for up to 5 days.

Coconut jam slice

This more-ish slice is as simple as they come. Pop a piece in the kids' lunchboxes or serve it for morning or afternoon tea, or warm with cream for dessert. Use your favourite jam — mixed berry, blackberry and apricot will all work well, and even orange marmalade can be used.

MAKES about 12 pieces **PREPARATION TIME** 20 minutes (+10 minutes chilling, and cooling)
COOKING TIME 35 minutes

150 g (5½ oz/1 cup) plain
(all-purpose) flour
75 g (2¾ oz/½ cup) self-raising
flour
60 g (2¼ oz/½ cup) icing
(confectioners') sugar
150 g (5½ oz) chilled butter,
chopped
1 egg yolk
165 g (5¾ oz/½ cup) strawberry
or raspberry jam

TOPPING
110 g (3¾ oz/½ cup) caster
(superfine) sugar
3 eggs, at room temperature
270 g (9½ oz/3 cups) desiccated
coconut, toasted

1   Preheat the oven to 180°C (350°F/ Gas 4). Brush the base and sides of a shallow 18 x 28 cm (7 x 11¼ inch) tin with melted butter or oil. Line the base and two long sides with a piece of non-stick baking paper, cutting into the corners to fit and allowing the paper to extend above the sides.

2   Put the flours, icing sugar, butter and egg yolk in a food processor. Use the pulse button to process until the mixture starts to come together *(pic 1)*. Turn the dough out onto a lightly floured work surface and press together until smooth. Use your fingertips to press the dough evenly into the prepared tin *(pic 2)*. Refrigerate for 10 minutes. Bake for 15 minutes or until golden brown and cooked through. Transfer to a wire rack and allow to cool in the tin.

3   Spread the jam evenly over the cooled slice base in the tin.

4   To make the topping, put the sugar and eggs in a medium bowl and use a balloon whisk to whisk until combined. Stir in the coconut. Spread the topping evenly over the jam, pressing down with the back of a spoon *(pic 3)*. Bake for 20 minutes or until the topping is light golden. Transfer to a wire rack and allow to cool in the tin. Cut into squares or fingers to serve.

TIP Keep in an airtight
container for up to 5 days.

Choc-coconut slice

Coconut and cocoa is always a winning combination and this old-fashioned slice is no exception. A classic melt-and-mix recipe using cocoa rather than chocolate, it's a great option for cake stalls, fetes and fundraisers as it's easy to make and doesn't require any costly ingredients.

MAKES about 20 pieces   **PREPARATION TIME** 20 minutes   **COOKING TIME** 20 minutes

150 g (5½ oz/1 cup) plain (all-purpose) flour
40 g (1½ oz/⅓ cup) unsweetened cocoa powder
295 g (10½ oz/1⅓ cups) caster (superfine) sugar
135 g (4¾ oz/1½ cups) desiccated coconut
200 g (7 oz) butter, melted and cooled
½ teaspoon natural vanilla extract
2 eggs, at room temperature, lightly whisked
2 tablespoons desiccated coconut, extra, to decorate

ICING
155 g (5½ oz/1¼ cups) icing (confectioners') sugar
2 tablespoons unsweetened cocoa powder
30 g (1 oz) butter, softened
1 tablespoon hot water

1 Preheat the oven to 180°C (350°F/ Gas 4). Brush the base and sides of a shallow 18 x 28 cm (7 x 11¼ inch) tin with melted butter or oil, then line the base and two long sides with a piece of non-stick baking paper, extending over the sides.

2 Sift the flour and cocoa together into a medium bowl. Stir in the sugar and coconut and make a well in the centre. Add the melted butter, vanilla and egg and use a wooden spoon to stir until well combined (*pic 1*).

3 Spoon the mixture into the prepared tin and use the back of the spoon to press evenly over the base (*pic 2*). Bake for 20 minutes or until a skewer inserted into the centre comes out clean. Transfer to a wire rack and allow to cool in the tin.

4 To make the icing (frosting), sift the icing sugar and cocoa together into a small bowl. Add the butter and hot water and stir until smooth.

5 Use the paper to lift the slice from the tin. Use a palette knife to spread the icing over the surface and then sprinkle with the extra coconut. Set aside at room temperature until the icing sets. Cut into squares or fingers to serve.

1

2

3

TIP Keep in an airtight container for up to 5 days.

Date crumble slice

With a delicious caramel flavour teamed with dates and oats, this slice is warming and comforting. It's ideal for lunchboxes and to take on picnics, as it travels well.

MAKES about 20 pieces   **PREPARATION TIME** 20 minutes   **COOKING TIME** 50–55 minutes

300 g (10½ oz) pitted dried
dates, chopped
200 g (7 oz) butter, softened
220 g (7¾ oz/1 cup, firmly packed)
light brown sugar
260 g (9¼ oz/1¾ cups) plain
(all-purpose) flour
½ teaspoon bicarbonate of soda
(baking soda)
150 g (5½ oz/1½ cups) rolled
(porridge) oats

1   Preheat the oven to 180°C (350°F/ Gas 4). Brush the base and sides of a shallow 18 x 28 cm (7 x 11¼ inch) tin with melted butter or oil, then line the base and 2 long sides with a piece of non-stick baking paper, extending over the sides.

2   Put the dates and 250 ml (9 fl oz/ 1 cup) water in a small saucepan over medium–low heat and cook, stirring occasionally, for 15 minutes or until the water has been absorbed *(pic 1)*. Remove from the heat and cool to room temperature.

3   Use an electric mixer to beat the butter and sugar in a small bowl until pale and creamy. Transfer to a large bowl. Sift the flour and bicarbonate of soda together. Add to the butter mixture with the oats and use a wooden spoon to mix until combined *(pic 2)*.

4   Spoon half the crumble mixture into the prepared tin and use the back of the spoon to press evenly over the base. Spread evenly with the date mixture. Spoon the remaining crumble mixture over the top and use the back of the spoon to press down lightly to cover the date mixture *(pic 3)*. Bake for 35–40 minutes or until cooked and golden brown. Transfer to a wire rack and allow to cool in the tin. Cut into squares or fingers to serve.

TIP Keep in an airtight container for up to 5 days.

Cakes

Simple chocolate cake

SERVES 12   **PREPARATION TIME** 20 minutes (+ cooling)   **COOKING TIME** 50–55 minutes (+ 15 minutes chilling)

185 g (6½ oz) unsalted butter,
  softened
330 g (11½ oz/1½ cups) caster
  (superfine) sugar
1 teaspoon natural vanilla extract
3 eggs, at room temperature
260 g (9¼ oz/1¾ cups) self-raising
  flour
55 g (2 oz/½ cup) unsweetened
  cocoa powder
180 ml (6 fl oz/¾ cup) milk

CHOCOLATE CURLS
200 g (7 oz) block couverture
  milk chocolate (see tip), at
  room temperature

CHOCOLATE FROSTING
125 g (4½ oz) dark chocolate,
  chopped
40 g (1½ oz) butter, chopped
165 g (5¾ oz/1⅓ cups) icing
  (confectioners') sugar, sifted
2 tablespoons milk

1   Preheat the oven to 180°C (350°F/
Gas 4). Grease a round 22 cm
(8½ inch) cake tin and line the base
with non-stick baking paper.

2   Use an electric mixer to beat the
butter, sugar and vanilla in a medium
bowl until pale and creamy. Add the
eggs one at a time, beating well after
each addition. Transfer to a large bowl.

3   Sift the flour and cocoa together.
Use a spatula or large metal spoon to
fold in the flour mixture alternately
with the milk, in two separate batches
each. Stir until just combined and
almost smooth.

4   Spoon the mixture into the
prepared tin and smooth the surface
with the back of the spoon. Bake the
cake for 45–50 minutes or until
a skewer inserted into the centre
comes out clean. Leave in the tin for
10 minutes before turning out onto
a wire rack to cool.

5   Meanwhile, to make the chocolate
curls, use a vegetable peeler (see tip)
to shave curls from the chocolate
block *(pic 1)*. Use small strips of non-
stick baking paper as a barrier between
your hands and the chocolate to help
prevent it melting while you hold it.
Catch the curls on a plate or a piece
of non-stick baking paper and
refrigerate until required. (You can
do them directly over the frosted cake
if you prefer.)

6   To make the chocolate frosting,
put the chocolate and butter in a small
heatproof bowl over a saucepan of
simmering water (make sure the water
doesn't touch the base of the bowl).
Stir until melted and smooth. Remove
the bowl from the heat and gradually
stir in the icing sugar *(pic 2)* and milk
until the frosting is thick and smooth.
Refrigerate, stirring occasionally, for
15 minutes or until the frosting is
a thick, spreadable consistency.

7   Spread the top and sides of the
cooled cake with the frosting *(pic 3)*
and decorate with the chocolate curls.

TIPS Milk chocolate has a
higher content of fat solids
and is less brittle than dark
chocolate, so is better
suited to making curls. Dark
chocolate tends to flake.
The wider the blade on your
vegetable peeler, the larger
the curls will be.
  You can replace the
frosting with 1 quantity
of chocolate buttercream.
  Keep in an airtight
container for up to 4 days.

Vanilla butter cake

This is a handy, reliable basic cake recipe that can be easily adapted to create different flavours. Try our variations, and decorate with your choice of flavoured buttercream or glacé icing.

SERVES 12   **PREPARATION TIME** 25 minutes (+ cooling)   **COOKING TIME** 1 hour

200 g (7 oz) unsalted butter, softened slightly
220 g (7¾ oz/1 cup) caster (superfine) sugar
1 teaspoon natural vanilla extract
3 eggs, at room temperature
300 g (10½ oz/2 cups) self-raising flour, sifted
(5¼ fl oz/²/₃ cup) milk
1 quantity buttercream of your choice (citrus buttercream pictured)

1   Preheat the oven to 170°C (325°F/Gas 3). Grease a square 20 cm (8 inch) cake tin and line the base with non-stick baking paper.

2   Use an electric mixer to beat the butter, sugar and vanilla in a medium bowl until pale and creamy. Add the eggs one at a time, beating well after each addition *(pic 1)*. Use a large metal spoon or spatula to fold in the flour and milk until combined.

3   Spoon the mixture into the prepared tin and smooth the surface with the back of the spoon *(pic 2)*. Bake for 1 hour or until a skewer inserted into the centre of the cake comes out clean *(pic 3)*. Leave the cake in the tin for 5 minutes before turning out onto a wire rack to cool completely.

4   Spread the buttercream evenly over the top and sides of the cooled cake.

VARIATIONS

Lemon butter cake: Replace the vanilla extract with 1 teaspoon finely grated lemon zest and replace 2 tablespoons of the milk with 2 tablespoons of lemon juice.

Coffee butter cake: Omit the vanilla extract and replace 125 ml (4 fl oz/½ cup) of the milk with freshly brewed strong coffee. Sprinkle the cake with 35 g (1¼ oz/¼ cup) slivered almonds before baking.

TIPS   This cake can be baked in a round 22 cm (8½ inch) cake tin.
   Keep the cake, iced or un-iced, in an airtight container for up to 3 days.

Passionfruit genoise sponge

The genoise sponge is traditionally made in a tin with sloping sides (called a Genoise cake tin) and served dusted with icing sugar. However, it is often baked to be used for a decorated gâteau or celebration cake, in which case it is generally baked in two sandwich tins. In this case, you can ensure you have exactly half the mixture in each tin by dividing the mixture between the tins and then weighing the tins to make sure they are equal in weight.

SERVES 10–12   **PREPARATION TIME** 30 minutes   **COOKING TIME** 18–20 minutes

350 g (12 oz/2⅓ cups) plain
   (all-purpose) flour
8 eggs
220 g (7¾ oz/1 cup) caster
   (superfine) sugar
100 g (3½ oz) unsalted butter,
   melted and cooled
125 ml (4 fl oz/½ cup) thickened
   (whipping) cream, to serve

PASSIONFRUIT ICING (FROSTING)
180 g (6¼ oz/1½ cups) icing
   (confectioners') sugar, sifted
20 g (¾ oz) butter, melted
1½ tablespoons passionfruit pulp
1 tablespoon boiling water

1   Preheat the oven to 180°C (350°F/ Gas 4). Lightly grease two shallow 22 cm (8½ inch) round cake tins with melted butter. Line the bases with non-stick baking paper, then lightly grease the paper and dust the inside of the tins with a little flour, shaking off any excess.

2   Sift the flour three times onto a piece of baking paper. Put the eggs and sugar in a large heatproof bowl. Place the bowl over a saucepan of simmering water (make sure the water doesn't touch the base of the bowl), and use hand-held electric beaters to whisk on high speed for 8 minutes or until the mixture is very thick and pale and a ribbon trail forms when the beaters are lifted. Remove from the heat and whisk for a further 3 minutes.

3   Use a large metal spoon to quickly and lightly fold the butter and flour into the egg mixture until just combined.

4   Spread the mixture evenly into the tins. Bake for 18–20 minutes in the centre of the oven or until lightly golden and shrunk slightly from the side of the tins, and a skewer inserted in the centres of the cakes comes out clean. Leave in the tins for 5 minutes before turning out onto a wire rack to cool.

5   To make the passionfruit icing, put all the ingredients in a medium bowl and mix with a wooden spoon until smooth and well combined. Use a balloon whisk or hand-held electric beaters to whisk the cream until soft peaks form. Sandwich the cooled cakes with cream. Spread with passionfruit icing, allowing it to dribble down the sides. Serve immediately.

> **TIPS** You can also use a 25 cm (10 inch) Genoise cake tin (see introduction). Bake for 25 minutes.
>   This cake is best eaten on the day it is baked.

Rich fruit cake

MAKES 22 cm (8½ inch) cake   **PREPARATION TIME** 30 minutes (+ overnight soaking and cooling)
COOKING TIME 2 hours 15 minutes

160 g (5¾ oz) sultanas (golden raisins)

125 g (4½ oz) glacé apricots (see tip), finely chopped

100 g (3½ oz) glacé orange (see tip), finely chopped

100 g (3½ oz) pitted prunes, finely chopped

100 g (3½ oz) dried figs, finely chopped

100 g (3½ oz) glacé cherries, quartered

100 g (3½ oz) pitted dried dates, finely chopped

80 g (2¾ oz) currants

125 ml (4 fl oz/½ cup) rum or brandy

200 g (7 oz) unsalted butter, softened

150 g (5½ oz/⅔ cup, firmly packed) dark brown sugar

2 teaspoons finely grated orange zest

4 eggs, at room temperature

185 g (6½ oz/1¼ cups) plain (all-purpose) flour, sifted

110 g (6½ oz/¾ cup) self-raising flour, sifted

1 teaspoon mixed (pumpkin pie) spice

125 g (4½ oz) whole mixed nuts of your choice (such as blanched almonds, pecan halves and/or hazelnuts)

1 Combine all the fruit and the rum or brandy in a large bowl. Cover and set aside overnight to soak *(pic 1)*.

2 Preheat the oven to 150°C (300°F/Gas 2). Grease a round 22 cm (8½ inch) cake tin. Line with two layers of non-stick baking paper *(pic 2)*.

3 Use an electric mixer to beat the butter, sugar and orange zest in a medium bowl until just combined. Add the eggs one at a time, beating well after each addition. Use a spatula or large metal spoon to stir the butter mixture into the fruit mixture. Stir in the sifted flours and mixed spice until combined. Spread the mixture evenly into the tin and tap the tin on the bench to remove any large air pockets. Smooth the surface with the back of a spoon. Decorate the top of the cake with nuts.

4 Bake the cake in the centre of the oven for 2¼ hours or until a skewer inserted into the centre of the cake comes out clean. Check the cake after 1¾ hours and if it is browning too much on top, cover loosely with a piece of foil.

5 Remove from the oven, cover the top with non-stick baking paper, wrap firmly in foil to seal, then wrap the cake and tin in a clean tea towel (dish towel) *(pic 3)* and leave to cool. (This will help the cake remain moist.) Unwrap and remove from the tin when cooled.

TIPS Glacé orange and apricots can be found at health food stores. You can replace them with mixed peel (mixed candied citrus peel) and dried apricots, respectively, if you prefer.
   Keep cake, wrapped in foil, in an airtight container in a cool place for up to 6 weeks.

Pound cake

Traditionally, a pound cake is made using equal weights of flour, butter, sugar and eggs, which is a great help for those who need to make a cake by memory. This version has slightly different proportions, resulting in a buttery, moist cake that keeps well.

SERVES 8   **PREPARATION TIME** 25 minutes   **COOKING TIME** 50 minutes

185 g (6½ oz) unsalted butter,
    softened slightly
165 g (5½ oz/¾ cup) caster
    (superfine) sugar
1 teaspoon natural vanilla extract
3 eggs, at room temperature
100 g (3½ oz/⅔ cup) plain
    (all-purpose) flour
75 g (2¾ oz/½ cup) self-raising
    flour
60 ml (2 fl oz/¼ cup) milk
Icing (confectioners') sugar,
    to dust

1   Preheat oven to 180°C (350°F/ Gas 4). Grease an 8 x 19 cm (3¼ x 7½ inch) loaf (bar) tin with melted butter or oil and line the base and two long sides with a piece of non-stick baking paper, extending over the sides *(pic 1)*.

2   Use an electric mixer to beat the butter, sugar and vanilla in a mixing bowl until pale and creamy *(pic 2)*. Add the eggs one at a time, beating well after each addition. Transfer to a large bowl. Sift the flours together. Use a large metal spoon to fold in the sifted flours alternately with the milk, in two separate batches each, until just combined and smooth *(pic 3)*.

3   Spoon the mixture into the prepared tin and smooth the surface with the back of the spoon. Bake the cake for 45–50 minutes or until a skewer inserted into the centre comes out clean. Leave the cake in the tin for 10 minutes, then turn out onto a wire rack to cool. Serve lightly dusted with icing sugar.

VARIATION

Marble cake: At the end of step 2, divide the cake batter evenly among three bowls. Mix a few drops of pink food colouring into the first bowl and 1 tablespoon sifted unsweetened cocoa powder into the second bowl. Leave the third bowl plain. Drop spoonfuls of each mixture alternately into the prepared tin. Use a palette knife to lightly swirl the mixtures together. Bake as directed above. Dust the cooled cake with icing sugar or spread with 1 quantity of chocolate buttercream to serve.

TIP Keep in an airtight container for up to 4 days.

Upside-down banana cake

What makes this cake is its sticky, rich caramel topping that is created while it cooks, beautifully complementing the banana. Serve it warm with ice cream as a dessert or as it is as a decadent afternoon treat.

SERVES 8   **PREPARATION TIME** 25 minutes   **COOKING TIME** 45 minutes

125 g (4½ oz) unsalted butter, softened
230 g (8 oz/1¼ cups, lightly packed) light brown sugar
2 eggs
225 g (8 oz/1½ cups) self-raising flour
1 teaspoon baking powder
2 very ripe large bananas, mashed

BANANA TOPPING
50 g (1¾ oz) unsalted butter, melted
60 g (2¼ oz/⅓ cup, lightly packed) light brown sugar
6 ripe large bananas, halved lengthways

1   Preheat the oven to 180°C (350°F/Gas 4). Grease and then line the base and sides of a 20 cm (8 inch) round cake tin with non-stick baking paper.

2   To make the banana topping, pour the melted butter over the base of the prepared tin and sprinkle evenly with the sugar. Arrange the bananas, cut side down, in a single layer over the base of the tin, cutting to fit if necessary.

3   Use an electric mixer to beat the butter and sugar until pale and creamy. Add the eggs one at a time, beating well after each addition.

4   Sift the flour and baking powder together into a bowl. Use a large metal spoon to gently fold the flour into the butter mixture with the mashed banana until well combined.

5   Carefully spoon the batter over the banana slices in the cake tin, smoothing the surface. Bake for 45 minutes or until a skewer inserted into the centre of the cake comes out clean. Remove from the oven and leave to cool in the tin for 5 minutes, before turning out onto a serving plate. Serve warm or at room temperature.

> **TIP** Keep in an airtight container in a cool place for up to 1 day.

Flourless chocolate cake

This is quite a modern flourless chocolate cake, using only a small amount of hazelnut meal to give body, resulting in a mousse-like texture. As eggs are the main ingredient, this cake rises up during cooking and then collapses and cracks a little on standing. Serve it chilled with fresh berries.

SERVES 8–10   **PREPARATION TIME** 10 minutes (+ 3 hours chilling)   **COOKING TIME** 1 hour 10 minutes

300 g (10½ oz) dark chocolate (50% cocoa solids), chopped
150 g (5½ oz) unsalted butter, chopped
5 eggs, at room temperature, separated
55 g (2 oz/¼ cup) caster (superfine) sugar, plus 75 g (2¾ oz/⅓ cup), extra
60 ml (2 fl oz/¼ cup) milk
110 g (3¾ oz/1 cup) hazelnut meal
Unsweetened cocoa powder, to dust
125 g (4½ oz/1 cup) raspberries, to serve
Cream, to serve (optional)

1 Preheat the oven to 150°C (300°F/Gas 2). Grease a round 20 cm (8 inch) spring-form cake tin and line with non-stick baking paper, extending 5 cm (2 inches) above the side *(pic 1)*. (The collar will support the cake as it rises during cooking and then fall as it cools.)

2 Put the chocolate and butter in a heatproof bowl over a saucepan of simmering water (make sure the base of the bowl doesn't touch the water). Stir occasionally until melted and smooth. Remove the bowl from the pan and set aside.

3 Use an electric mixer with a whisk attachment to whisk the egg whites and sugar in a clean, dry medium bowl until stiff peaks form. Set aside.

4 Put the eggs yolks and the extra sugar in a medium mixing bowl and use a balloon whisk to whisk until thick and pale *(pic 2)*. Whisk in the milk. Add the chocolate mixture and hazelnut meal and whisk to combine. Use a spatula or large metal spoon to fold in one-third of the egg whites until just combined *(pic 3)*. Fold in the remaining egg whites in two more batches. Spoon into the prepared tin and smooth the surface.

5 Bake for 45 minutes without opening the oven door. Turn the cake tin around to ensure even cooking and bake for a further 20 minutes or until the top of the cake feels set. Transfer to a wire rack and cool in the tin. Refrigerate for 3 hours or until well chilled.

6 Cut away the excess paper from around the side of the tin. Invert the cake onto a plate and remove the baking paper. Gently place a serving plate on top and turn the cake the right way up. Use a fine sieve to dust with cocoa powder. Use a sharp knife, dipped in very hot water and then dried, to cut the cake into slices. Serve accompanied by raspberries and cream, if desired.

TIP Keep in an airtight container in the refrigerator for up to 4 days.

White chocolate mud cake

SERVES 16–20   **PREPARATION TIME** 20 minutes (+ cooling and 4 hours chilling)   **COOKING TIME** 1 hour 15 minutes

250 g (9 oz) white chocolate,
   chopped
200 g (7 oz) butter, chopped
330 g (11½ oz/1½ cups) caster
   (superfine) sugar
2 eggs, at room temperature
1 teaspoon natural vanilla extract
150 g (5½ oz/1 cup) plain
   (all-purpose) flour
150 g (5½ oz/1 cup) self-raising
   flour
1 quantity white chocolate
   buttercream

1   Preheat the oven to 160°C (315°F/
Gas 2–3). Grease a deep, square 20 cm
(8 inch) cake tin and line the base and
sides with non-stick baking paper.

2   Put the chocolate, butter and
200 ml (7 fl oz) water in a medium
saucepan. Stir over low heat until
melted and well combined. Transfer
to a large bowl, stir in the sugar
and set aside until the mixture is
lukewarm.

3   Add the eggs and vanilla to the
chocolate mixture and use a balloon
whisk to whisk until just combined.
Sift the flours together over the
chocolate mixture and stir with the
whisk until smooth *(pic 1)*. Pour into
the prepared tin and tap gently on the
bench to settle the mixture.

4   Bake for 1 hour 10 minutes,
turning the tin around halfway
through cooking to ensure even
cooking, or until a skewer inserted
into the centre of the cake comes
out clean. (The top of the cake might
crack slightly as it nears the end of
the cooking time.) Cool the cake in
the tin placed on a wire rack for
15 minutes, then turn it out onto
the wire rack and cool completely.
Remove the cake from the tin,
wrap in plastic wrap and place in
the refrigerator for 4 hours or until
well chilled. This will make icing
(frosting) the cake easier.

5   Use a sharp serrated knife to trim
the top of the cake if you wish *(pic 2)*.
Use a pastry brush to brush away any
crumbs. Place the cake upside-down
on a serving plate or cake stand. Use
a palette knife to spread the white
chocolate buttercream over the top
and sides of the cake *(pic 3)*.

1

2

3

TIPS Don't use a non-stick
pan for this cake, as the crust
will become too dark due to
the extended cooking time.
   Keep in an airtight
container in the refrigerator
for up to 4 days. Remove
from the refrigerator up to
1 hour before serving to
bring to room temperature.

Glacé fruit and nut loaf

SERVES 12–16   **PREPARATION TIME** 30 minutes (+ cooling)   **COOKING TIME** 1 hour 45 minutes

50 g (1¾ oz) unsalted butter, softened

60 g (2¼ oz/⅓ cup, lightly packed) light brown sugar

2 tablespoons breakfast marmalade

2 eggs, lightly whisked

150 g (5½ oz/1 cup) plain (all-purpose) flour

1 teaspoon baking powder

1 teaspoon ground nutmeg

225 g (8 oz/1¼ cups) pitted dates, chopped

240 g (8¾ oz/1½ cups) raisins

155 g (5½ oz/1 cup) brazil nuts

140 g (5 oz/⅔ cup) mixed red, yellow and green glacé cherries

110 g (3¾ oz/½ cup) chopped glacé pear or pineapple

120 g (4¼ oz/½ cup) chopped glacé apricots

120 g (4¼ oz/½ cup) chopped glacé peaches

120 g (4¼ oz/⅓ cup) chopped glacé figs

100 g (3½ oz/1 cup) walnut halves

100 g (3½ oz/⅔ cup) blanched almonds

TOPPING

2 tablespoons breakfast marmalade

2 teaspoons powdered gelatine

150 g (5½ oz) glacé pineapple or pear rings, cut into eighths

100 g (3½ oz) red, yellow and green glacé cherries

40 g (1½ oz/¼ cup) blanched almonds

1   Preheat the oven to 150°C (300°F/Gas 2). Lightly grease and line a deep 8 x 20.5 cm (3¼ x 8¼ inch) loaf (bar) tin. Line a baking tray with several layers of newspaper.

2   Use an electric mixer to beat the butter, sugar and marmalade in a mxiing bowl until pale and creamy. Add the egg gradually, beating thoroughly after each addition.

3   Sift the flour, baking powder and nutmeg together into a large bowl. Add the fruit and nuts and mix until each piece is coated in the flour mixture. Add to the egg mixture and use a wooden spoon to mix to combine well.

4   Spoon the mixture into the prepared tin, pushing well into the corners. Wrap layers of newspaper around the outside of the tin (see page 22) and sit the cake tin on the lined baking tray. Bake for 1½–1¾ hours or until a skewer inserted into the centre of the cake comes out clean. Cool in the tin for 30 minutes, then turn out onto a wire rack to cool.

5   To make the topping, mix the marmalade with 2 tablespoons water in a small heatproof bowl. Sprinkle with gelatine. Bring a saucepan of water to the boil, then remove from the heat. Stand the bowl in the pan and stir until the gelatine has dissolved. Brush the top of the cake with some of the gelatine mixture and arrange the pineapple pieces, cherries and almonds on top. Brush with a little more gelatine mixture and allow to set.

TIPS You can toast the blanched almonds for the topping if you wish. To do this, spread them in a single layer on a baking tray and bake in a 180°C (350°F/Gas 4) oven for 8 minutes or until lightly golden.

Keep in an airtight container for up to 1 week

Honey roll

The key to a good Swiss roll-type cake is not to overcook the cake. To avoid cracking, make sure the work surface you turn the sponge cake on to isn't too cold, and work quickly so the cake is still warm when you roll it up the first time.

SERVES 8   **PREPARATION TIME** 25 minutes (+ cooling)   **COOKING TIME** 12 minutes

110 g (3¾ oz/¾ cup) self-raising flour
2 teaspoons mixed (pumpkin pie) spice
3 eggs
125 g (4½ oz/⅔ cup, lightly packed) light brown sugar
25 g (1 oz/¼ cup) desiccated coconut

HONEY CREAM
125 g (4½ oz) unsalted butter, softened
80 g (2¾ oz/⅓ cup) caster (superfine) sugar
2 tablespoons honey

1   Preheat the oven to 210°C (415°F/ Gas 6–7). Grease a 25 x 30 cm (10 x 12 inch) Swiss roll (jelly roll) tin and line with non-stick baking paper.

2   Sift the flour and mixed spice together onto a large sheet of baking paper three times.

3   Use an electric mixer with a whisk attachment to whisk the eggs in a large bowl for 5 minutes or until pale. Add the sugar gradually, beating constantly until the sugar has dissolved and the mixture is very thick and pale. Use a large metal spoon to gently fold in the sifted flour mixture until just combined and almost smooth.

4   Spoon the batter into the prepared tin, gently smoothing the surface. Bake for 12 minutes or until lightly golden and springy to the touch. Remove from the oven and leave to cool in the tin for 1 minute.

5   Lay a clean, dry tea towel (dish towel) on a work surface. Cover with a sheet of non-stick baking paper, then sprinkle the coconut over the paper. Turn the cake onto the coconut and leave for 1 minute.

6   Using the paper as a guide, carefully roll the cake, along with the paper, starting at a short side. Set aside on a wire rack until cool, then unroll the cake and discard the paper.

7   To make the honey cream, use electric beaters to beat the butter, sugar and honey in a small bowl until light and fluffy. Continue beating for 12 minutes, adding a teaspoon of cold water every 2 minutes.

8   Unroll the cake, spread evenly with the honey cream and then gently but firmly re-roll using the paper as a guide. Use a sharp knife to trim the ends. Cut into slices just before serving.

> **TIP** Keep, wrapped in non-stick baking paper, in an airtight container in a cool place for up to 2 days.

Coffee and walnut cake

Coffee and walnuts are a gorgeous combination, and this cake is good proof. It's a straightforward melt-and-mix cake, so there's no beating, no whisking and no special equipment required, and it takes very little preparation to get it into the oven.

SERVES 8–10   **PREPARATION TIME** 10 minutes (+ cooling)   **COOKING TIME** 45 minutes

125 ml (4 fl oz/½ cup) milk
75 g (2¾ oz) butter, chopped
1 tablespoon instant coffee granules
110 g (3¾ oz/½ cup) caster (superfine) sugar
60 g (2¼ oz/½ cup) coarsely chopped walnuts, plus walnut halves, extra, to decorate
1 egg, at room temperature, lightly whisked
150 g (5½ oz/1 cup) self-raising flour, sifted
⅔ quantity coffee buttercream (see page 14)

1 Preheat the oven to 160°C (315°F/ Gas 2–3). Grease an 8 x 19 cm (3¼ x 7½ inch) loaf (bar) tin and line the base and two long sides with one piece of non-stick baking paper, extending over the sides.

2 Put the milk, butter and coffee in a large saucepan over medium–high heat. Stir for 2 minutes or until the butter melts and the coffee dissolves *(pic 1)*. Remove from the heat. Use a wooden spoon to stir in the sugar and walnuts. Stir in the egg until combined. Stir in the flour until just combined *(pic 2)*.

3 Pour the mixture into the prepared tin and smooth the surface with the back of a spoon. Bake for 40 minutes or until a skewer inserted into the centre of the cake comes out clean. Cool in the tin for 5 minutes, then turn onto a wire rack to cool completely.

4 Spread the top of the cake with coffee buttercream *(pic 3)* and decorate with extra walnut halves.

1

2

3

TIP Keep in an airtight container for up to 3 days.

Semolina lemon syrup cake

Pouring an intensely sweet syrup over a cake after cooking not only adds extra sweetness and flavour but also results in an incredibly moist cake that keeps well. The semolina in this cake also adds a lovely texture that prevents it from going soggy once the syrup is soaked up.

MAKES about 20 pieces   **PREPARATION TIME** 20 minutes   **COOKING TIME** 1 hour

125 g (4½ oz) unsalted butter, softened
185 g (6½ oz/¾ cup) caster (superfine) sugar
2 teaspoons finely grated lemon zest
3 eggs
185 g (6½ oz/1½ cups) semolina
150 g (5½ oz/1 cup) self-raising flour
125 ml (4 fl oz/½ cup) milk
80 g (2¾ oz/½ cup) blanched almonds, toasted and finely chopped
Flaked almonds, to decorate

SYRUP
625 g (1 lb 6 oz/2½ cups) sugar
2 tablespoons lemon juice

1   Preheat the oven to 170°C (325°F/ Gas 3). Lightly grease a shallow 18 x 28 cm (7 x 11¼ inch) cake tin.

2   To make the syrup, dissolve the sugar in 750 ml (26 fl oz/3 cups) water in a saucepan over high heat. Add the lemon juice and bring to the boil, then reduce the heat and simmer for 20 minutes. Remove from the heat and allow to cool.

3   Meanwhile, use an electric mixer to beat the butter, caster sugar and zest until pale and creamy. Add the eggs one at a time, beating well after each addition.

4   Sift the semolina and flour together and fold into the butter mixture alternately with the milk. Mix in the chopped almonds, then spread the mixture into the tin and arrange rows of flaked almonds on top.

5   Bake for 35–40 minutes or until it is golden and shrinks slightly from the sides of the tin. Prick the surface with a fine skewer, then pour the cooled syrup over the hot cake. Cool in the tin before cutting it into squares or diamonds to serve.

> **TIP** Keep in an airtight container for up to 5 days.

Cupcakes

There are two great things about cupcakes: they're single portions and therefore ready to serve, and they are open to myriad flavouring and decorating options. This simple recipe is the perfect starting point for a foray into cupcakes, complete with variations in flavour and decorating ideas for inspiration.

MAKES 12   **PREPARATION TIME** 15 minutes   **COOKING TIME** 18–20 minutes

225 g (8 oz/1½ cups) plain
    (all-purpose) flour
1½ teaspoons baking powder
150 g (5½ oz/²⁄₃ cup) caster
    (superfine) sugar
125 g (4½ oz) unsalted butter,
    softened
60 ml (2 fl oz/¼ cup) milk
3 eggs, at room temperature
1 teaspoon natural vanilla extract
Icing (frosting) and decorations of
    your choice (see suggestions
    below)

1   Preheat the oven to 170°C (325°F/ Gas 3). Line twelve 80 ml (2½ fl oz/ ⅓ cup) muffin tin holes with paper cases.

2   Sift the flour and baking powder together into a mixing bowl. Add the sugar, butter, milk, eggs and vanilla *(pic 1)*. Use an electric mixer to beat on low speed until combined. Increase speed to medium and beat for 3 minutes or until well combined and paler in colour *(pic 2)*. Divide the mixture evenly among the cases.

3   Bake for 18–20 minutes or until golden and a skewer inserted into the centre of the cakes comes out clean. Cool for 5 minutes in the tin, then transfer to a wire rack to cool completely *(pic 3)*.

4   Spread the cupcakes with icing and finish with decorations of your choice.

DECORATING IDEAS

Lemon daisy cupcakes: Ice 12 cupcakes with 1 quantity citrus glacé icing (frosting). Cut 15 white marshmallows in half crossways, then in half lengthways. Arrange the marshmallow quarters, cut side up, on the cakes to make flower shapes. Place a yellow jelly bean in the centre of each marshmallow flower.

Vanilla sparkle cupcakes: Put 1 quantity vanilla buttercream in a piping (icing) bag fitted with a 1 cm (½ inch) star nozzle. Pipe a large circle in the centre of a cupcake. Then, starting near the outside edge of the cupcake, generously pipe a swirl around and over the circle. Sprinkle with silver cachous or sprinkles of your choice. Repeat with the remaining buttercream, sprinkles and cupcakes.

Strawberries and cream cupcakes: Spread 12 cupcakes with 1 quantity vanilla buttercream. Hull 12 medium strawberries and thinly slice lengthways. Arrange the strawberry slices, overlapping slightly, on each cupcake. Melt 2 tablespoons strawberry jam and 1 tablespoon water in a small saucepan and use a pastry brush to brush over the strawberries.

1

2

3

> **TIPS** Keep iced cupcakes in an airtight container in the refrigerator for up to 2 days. Remove from the refrigerator 15–30 minutes before serving to bring to room temperature.

Madeleines

Small, delicate and deliciously buttery, madeleines are cooked in special tins to give them their characteristic shell shape. Eat them straight from the oven while the inside is still warm and sponge-like and the outside is more-ishly crisp.

MAKES 12   **PREPARATION TIME** 20 minutes   **COOKING TIME** 12 minutes

150 g (5½ oz/1 cup) plain (all-purpose) flour, plus extra to dust
2 eggs
170 g (5¾ oz/¾ cup) caster (superfine) sugar
185 g (6½ oz) unsalted butter, melted and cooled, plus extra, to grease
1 teaspoon finely grated orange zest (see tip)
2 tablespoons icing (confectioners') sugar, to dust

1   Preheat the oven to 180°C (350°F/ Gas 4). Grease a 12-hole madeleine tin or shallow patty pan with extra melted butter. Lightly dust the tin with flour and shake off any excess.

2   Sift the flour three times onto non-stick baking paper. Combine the eggs and sugar in a heatproof bowl. Place over a saucepan of simmering water (make sure the water doesn't touch the base of the bowl) and use hand-held electric beaters to whisk until very thick and pale yellow and a ribbon trail forms when the beaters are lifted. Remove the bowl from the saucepan and continue to beat the mixture until it has cooled slightly and increased in volume.

3   Add the sifted flour, butter and orange zest to the bowl and use a large metal spoon or spatula to quickly and lightly fold in until just combined.

4   Spoon the mixture carefully into the madeleine holes and bake for 10–12 minutes or until lightly golden. Stand for 2 minutes in tins. Carefully remove from the tin and transfer to a wire rack. Dust with icing sugar before serving.

TIPS Mandarin, lemon or lime zest can be used in place of the orange zest.

These madeleines are best eaten on the day they are baked.

Blueberry and almond friands

Friands are small cakes made with almond meal and whisked egg white that are based on the French financier (interestingly, a French friand is a sausage roll). They're a breeze to make, as all the ingredients are simply folded into the whisked egg whites and then baked.

MAKES 12   **PREPARATION TIME** 15 minutes   **COOKING TIME** 20 minutes

6 egg whites, at room temperature
160 g (5¾ oz) butter, melted and
   cooled
250 g (9 oz/2 cups) icing
   (confectioners') sugar
125 g (4½ oz/1¼ cups) almond meal
100 g (3½ oz/²/₃ cup) plain
   (all-purpose) flour
150 g (5½ oz) frozen blueberries
20 g (¾ oz/¼ cup) flaked almonds

1　Preheat the oven to 200°C (400°F/ Gas 6). Lightly grease a 12-hole friand tin (see tips) with melted butter.

2　Use a balloon whisk to whisk the egg whites in a medium bowl until frothy but not firm *(pic 1)*. Use a wooden spoon to stir in the butter, icing sugar, almond meal and flour until just combined. Quickly stir through the frozen blueberries *(pic 2)*.

3　Divide the mixture evenly among the greased friand holes and sprinkle with flaked almonds *(pic 3)*.

4　Bake for 20 minutes or until a skewer inserted into the centre of a friand comes out clean. Cool in the tin for 5 minutes, then turn out onto a wire rack to cool.

VARIATIONS

Raspberry and pistachio friands: Replace the blueberries with frozen raspberries and the flaked almonds with roughly chopped pistachios.

Cherry and hazelnut friands: Replace the almond meal with ground hazelnuts and the blueberries with frozen cherries. Omit the flaked almonds.

1

2

3

TIPS Friand tins are available from large supermarkets and kitchenware stores.
   You can also use a 12-hole 80 ml (2½ fl oz/¹/₃ cup) muffin tin.
   Keep in an airtight container for up to 4 days.

Nectarine and almond cake

This is one of those fabulously no-fuss cakes you will come back to time and again. Mixing the cake batter with a food processor makes it quick and easy, then all you have to do is layer it with the fruit and nuts in the tin. For a quick dessert, serve it warm with pouring (whipping) cream or ice cream.

SERVES 8 **PREPARATION TIME** 15 minutes **COOKING TIME** 50 minutes

150 g (5½ oz/1 cup) plain
(all-purpose) flour
110 g (3¾ oz/½ cup) caster
(superfine) sugar
1 teaspoon baking powder
2 teaspoons finely grated lemon zest
125 g (4½ oz) chilled unsalted
butter, diced
2 eggs, at room temperature
35 g (1¼ oz/⅓ cup) flaked almonds
4 yellow nectarines, about 450 g
(1 lb), each cut into 12 wedges
Icing (confectioners') sugar, to dust
(optional)
Pouring (whipping) cream or vanilla
ice cream, to serve (optional)

1 Preheat the oven to 180°C (350°F/ Gas 4). Grease a round 20 cm (8 inch) spring-form cake tin well with butter.

2 Put the flour, caster sugar, baking powder and lemon zest in a food processor and process until well combined. Add the butter and process until the mixture resembles fine breadcrumbs *(pic 1)*. With the motor running, add the eggs and process using the pulse button until the mixture is just combined.

3 Spread half the mixture evenly into the greased tin. Sprinkle with half the almonds and top with half the nectarines *(pic 2)*. Cover with the remaining batter, smoothing the surface with the spatula *(pic 3)*. Arrange the remaining nectarines on top and sprinkle with the remaining almonds.

4 Bake for 50 minutes or until golden and a skewer inserted into the centre of the cake comes out clean. Leave in the tin for 5 minutes, then remove and transfer the cake to a wire rack to cool.

5 Serve either warm or at room temperature, dusted with icing sugar and accompanied by cream or ice cream, if desired.

TIPS You can vary the fruit and nuts depending on the season. In autumn, try apple and pine nuts or pear and almonds.
Keep in an airtight container for up to 3 days.

Muffins,
Scones &
Quick Breads

Banana muffins

This is a good, reliable recipe from which to build your muffin repertoire. Once you've mastered this recipe, try our variations and let them inspire you to create other flavour combinations.

MAKES 12   **PREPARATION TIME** 15 minutes   **COOKING TIME** 20–25 minutes

300 g (10½ oz/2 cups) self-raising
   flour
½ teaspoon ground cinnamon
   or nutmeg
110 g (3¾ oz/½ cup, firmly packed)
   light brown sugar
125 ml (4 fl oz/½ cup) milk
2 eggs, at room temperature,
   lightly whisked
1 teaspoon natural vanilla extract
300 g (10½ oz/1¼ cups) mashed
   very ripe banana (see tip)
125 g (4½ oz) butter, melted
   and cooled
60 g (2¼ oz/½ cup) pecan or
   walnut halves, coarsely chopped,
   to sprinkle

1   Preheat the oven to 180°C (350°F/ Gas 4). Lightly brush twelve 80 ml (2½ fl oz/⅓ cup) muffin holes with melted butter to grease.

2   Sift the flour and cinnamon or nutmeg together into a large bowl. Stir in the sugar, then make a well in the centre.

3   Whisk the milk, egg and vanilla together in a jug *(pic 1)*, then pour into the well. Add the mashed banana and melted butter. Use a large metal spoon to fold together until just combined but not smooth *(pic 2)*. (Do not overmix or the muffins will be tough — the batter should still be a little lumpy.)

4   Divide the mixture evenly among the muffin holes and sprinkle with the nuts. Bake for 20–25 minutes or until the muffins are golden and a skewer inserted into the centre comes out clean. Leave in the tin for 3 minutes, then use a palette knife to release each muffin from the tin and lift out *(pic 3)*. Cool on a wire rack and serve at room temperature.

VARIATIONS

Chocolate muffins: Omit the spice, banana and nuts. Replace 75 g (2¾ oz/½ cup) of the flour with 55 g (2 oz/½ cup) unsweetened cocoa powder and increase the milk to 185 ml (6 fl oz/¾ cup).

Orange muffins: Omit the spice, banana and nuts. Replace the brown sugar with 110 g (3¾ oz/½ cup) caster (superfine) sugar. Replace the milk with 185 ml (6 fl oz/¾ cup) buttermilk. Replace the vanilla with 1 tablespoon finely grated orange zest.

1

2

3

TIPS You'll need 3 very ripe medium bananas for this recipe.
   Keep in an airtight container for up to 2 days. To freeze, wrap individually in plastic wrap, then put in a freezer bag or airtight container. Seal, label, date and freeze for up to 3 months. Thaw at room temperature.

White chocolate and blackberry muffins

Berries are a terrific addition to muffin batters, and when chocolate is also put in the mix the results are heavenly. If you can't find blackberries, use blueberries or raspberries, and if you are using frozen berries, don't thaw them or they will streak the batter. Dark chocolate works just as well as white.

MAKES 12   **PREPARATION TIME** 20 minutes   **COOKING TIME** 25–30 minutes

375 g (13 oz/2½ cups) self-raising
   flour
200 g (7 oz) white chocolate,
   chopped
125 g (4½ oz) butter
110 g (3¾ oz/½ cup, firmly packed)
   light brown sugar
125 ml (4 fl oz/½ cup) milk
3 eggs, at room temperature
300 g (10½ oz/2⅓ cups) fresh or
   frozen blackberries
2 tablespoons sugar, to sprinkle

1   Preheat the oven to 180°C (350°F/
Gas 4). Lightly brush twelve 80 ml
(2½ fl oz/⅓ cup) muffin holes with oil
or melted butter to grease.

2   Sift the flour into a bowl and
stir in 125 g (4½ oz) of the chocolate.
Make a well in the centre.

3   Place the remaining chocolate
and the butter in a medium heatproof
bowl over a saucepan of simmering
water (make sure the base of the bowl
doesn't touch the water). Stir until
melted and combined (*pic 1*). Remove
the bowl from the pan, add the brown
sugar and milk and stir with a balloon
whisk until well combined. Whisk in
the eggs.

4   Add the butter mixture to the
flour mixture and use a spatula or
large metal spoon to gently fold
together until just combined but not
smooth. Gently stir in the blackberries
(*pic 2*). (Do not overmix or the muffins
will be tough — the batter should still
be a little lumpy.)

5   Divide the mixture evenly among
the muffin holes (*pic 3*). Sprinkle with
the sugar. Bake for 20–25 minutes
or until the muffins are risen, golden
and come away slightly from the side
of the tin. Leave in the tin for
3 minutes, then use a palette knife
to release each muffin from the tin
and lift out. Cool on a wire rack and
serve at room temperature.

1

2

3

TIP Keep in an airtight
container for up to 2 days.
   To freeze, wrap individually
in plastic wrap, then put
in a freezer bag or airtight
container. Seal, label,
date and freeze for up to 3
months. Thaw the muffins
at room temperature.

Spinach and feta muffins

Savoury muffins make a great snack for lunchboxes or to take on picnics, or you can serve them with a warming bowl of soup. They are also delicious served warm with lashings of butter. You can replace the feta in this recipe with haloumi, cut into small pieces, if you prefer.

MAKES 12   **PREPARATION TIME** 20 minutes   **COOKING TIME** 25 minutes

250 g (9 oz) frozen spinach, thawed
335 g (11¾ oz/2¼ cups) self-raising flour
200 g (7 oz) feta cheese, crumbled
100 g (3½ oz/1¼ cups) finely shredded parmesan cheese
250 ml (9 fl oz/1 cup) milk
2 eggs, at room temperature
125 g (4½ oz) butter, melted and cooled

1   Preheat the oven to 190°C (375°F/ Gas 5). Lightly brush twelve 80 ml (2½ fl oz/⅓ cup) muffin holes with oil or melted butter.

2   Use your hands to squeeze as much moisture as you can from the spinach (pic 1), then finely chop it.

3   Sift the flour into a bowl and season well with freshly ground black pepper. Stir in half each of the feta and parmesan, then make a well in the centre. Whisk the milk and eggs together in a jug, then pour into the well. Add the melted butter (pic 2). Use a spatula or large metal spoon to gently fold together until just combined but not smooth. Stir in the spinach. (Do not overmix or the muffins will be tough — the batter should still be a little lumpy.)

4   Fill each muffin hole three-quarters full. Mix together the remaining cheeses and sprinkle over each muffin (pic 3).

5   Bake for 25 minutes or until golden and a skewer inserted into the centre of a muffin comes out clean. As soon as you remove them from the oven, use a palette knife to release each muffin from the tin and transfer to a wire rack. Serve the muffins warm.

1

2

3

> **TIP**   Keep in an airtight container for up to 2 days. To freeze, wrap individually in plastic wrap, then put in a freezer bag or airtight container. Seal, label, date and freeze for up to 3 months. Thaw the muffins at room temperature.

Plain scones

Scones are the cornerstone of all good baking repertoires. The techniques of rubbing in and mixing with a flat-bladed knife are both required, and if done with a light touch will produce light, fluffy scones. This recipe will have you whipping up a perfect batch of scones in just under half an hour.

MAKES about 9   **PREPARATION TIME** 15 minutes   **COOKING TIME** 10–12 minutes

375 g (13 oz/2½ cups) self-raising
    flour, plus extra, to dust
    (optional)
1 teaspoon baking powder
Pinch of salt
60 g (2¼ oz) chilled butter, chopped
250 ml (9 fl oz/1 cup) milk,
    plus extra, to glaze
Butter and jam, to serve

1   Preheat the oven to 220°C (425°F/ Gas 7). Lightly grease a baking tray or line with non-stick baking paper.

2   Sift the flour, baking powder and salt together into a medium mixing bowl. With your palms facing upwards, use your fingertips to rub in the butter *(pic 1)* until the mixture resembles fine breadcrumbs. Make a well in the centre.

3   Add almost all the milk and mix with a flat-bladed knife, using a cutting action, until the dough comes together in clumps *(pic 2)*. Mix to a soft dough, adding the remaining milk if necessary.

4   Use lightly floured hands to gently gather the dough, lift it onto a lightly floured work surface and knead very lightly and briefly to bring it together into a smooth ball. Pat the dough out to 2.5 cm (1 inch) thick. Use a floured round 6–7 cm (2½–2¾ inch) cutter to cut out scones, pressing straight down on the cutter and not twisting it (see tip). Gather the dough trimmings

together and, without handling them too much, press out again to a 2.5 cm (1 inch) thickness and cut out more rounds. Place the scones close together on the prepared tray. Brush lightly with the extra milk *(pic 3)* and dust lightly with extra flour, if desired.

5   Bake the scones for 10–12 minutes or until they are well risen, golden brown on top and sound hollow when tapped on the base. Serve warm or at room temperature, with butter and jam.

VARIATIONS

Sultana scones: Stir 85 g (3 oz/½ cup) sultanas (golden raisins) into the flour mixture before adding the milk.

Date scones: Stir 150 g (5½ oz) fresh dates, pitted and chopped, into the flour mixture before adding the milk.

Buttermilk scones: Use buttermilk instead of the milk.

Cheese scones: Stir 50 g (1¾ oz/ ½ cup, loosely packed) coarsely grated cheddar cheese and 25 g (1¼ oz/ ¼ cup) finely grated parmesan cheese into the flour mixture before adding the milk. Sprinkle the scones with 25 g (1 oz/¼ cup, loosely packed) coarsely grated cheddar cheese after brushing with the extra milk.

TIPS If you twist the cutter when cutting out the scones, the scones will rise unevenly. To keep the scones warm, wrap in a clean tea towel (dish towel).
    These scones are best eaten on the day they are baked.

Rich scones

These scones are enriched by the addition of an egg and cream instead of milk, making their texture wonderfully tender and light. They are delicious served simply with good-quality butter or teamed with cream and berry jam, honey or even golden syrup.

MAKES about 10   **PREPARATION TIME** 15 minutes   **COOKING TIME** 10–12 minutes

300 g (10½ oz/2 cups) self-raising
   flour
1 teaspoon baking powder
Pinch of salt
40 g (1½ oz) chilled butter, chopped
55 g (2 oz/¼ cup) caster
   (superfine) sugar
1 egg, at room temperature
185 ml (6 fl oz/¾ cup) pouring
   (whipping) cream
½ teaspoon natural vanilla extract
1 egg, lightly whisked, to glaze
Jam and whipped cream, to serve
   (optional)

1   Preheat the oven to 220°C (425°F/ Gas 7). Lightly grease a baking tray or line with non-stick baking paper.

2   Sift the flour, baking powder and salt together into a medium mixing bowl. With your palms facing upwards, use your fingertips to rub in the butter until the mixture resembles fine breadcrumbs. Stir in the sugar and make a well in the centre *(pic 1)*.

3   Whisk the egg, cream and vanilla together with a fork. Add to the dry ingredients and mix with a flat-bladed knife, using a cutting action, until the dough comes together in clumps.

4   Use lightly floured hands to gently gather the dough, lift it onto a lightly floured work surface and knead very lightly and briefly to bring it together into a smooth ball *(pic 2)*. Pat the dough out to 2.5 cm (1 inch) thick. Use a floured round 6–7 cm (2½–2¾ inch) cutter to cut out scones, pressing straight down on the cutter and not twisting it *(pic 3)*. Gather the dough trimmings together and, without handling them too much, press out again to a 2.5 cm (1 inch) thickness and cut out more rounds. Place the scones close together on the prepared tray and brush lightly with the whisked egg.

5   Bake the scones for 10–12 minutes or until they are well risen, golden brown on top and sound hollow when tapped on the base. Serve warm with jam and cream, if desired.

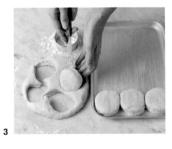

TIP These scones are best eaten on the day they are baked.

Cheese scones

Savoury scones, such as these cheese ones, make a perfect accompaniment to wintery soups and slow-cooked casseroles and stews. Serve them straight from the oven to mop up the juices. They are also delicious as a snack with lashings of butter.

MAKES 12   **PREPARATION TIME** 15 minutes   **COOKING TIME** 12–15 minutes

300 g (10½ oz/2 cups) self-raising flour
1 teaspoon baking powder
½ teaspoon mustard powder
30 g (1 oz) chilled butter, chopped
25 g (1 oz/¼ cup) finely grated parmesan cheese
90 g (3¼ oz/¾ cup) finely grated cheddar cheese
250 ml (9 fl oz/1 cup) milk

1   Preheat the oven to 220°C (425°F/Gas 7). Lightly grease a baking tray or line with non-stick baking paper.

2   Sift the flour, baking powder, mustard and a pinch of salt together into a medium mixing bowl. With your palms facing upwards, use your fingertips to rub in the butter until mixture resembles fine breadcrumbs. Stir in parmesan and 60 g (2¼ oz/½ cup) of the cheddar, making sure they don't clump together. Make a well in the centre.

3   Add almost all the milk and mix with a flat-bladed knife, using a cutting action, until the dough comes together in clumps. Mix to a soft dough, adding the remaining milk if necessary.

4   Use lightly floured hands to gently gather the dough, lift it onto a lightly floured work surface and knead very lightly and briefly to bring it together into a smooth ball. Pat the dough out to 2 cm (¾ inch) thick. Use a floured round 5 cm (2 inch) cutter to cut out scones, pressing straight down on the cutter and not twisting it. Gather the dough trimmings together and, without handling them too much, press out again to a 2 cm (¾ inch) thickness and cut out more rounds. Place the scones close together on the prepared tray and sprinkle with the remaining cheese.

5   Bake the scones for 12–15 minutes or until they are well risen, golden brown on top and sound hollow when tapped on the base. Serve warm or at room temperature.

TIP These scones are best eaten on the day they are baked.

Raspberry-filled scones

These scones have a clever twist. They're baked with a pocket of jam inside, so if you want to transport them all you need to take is some thick cream for dipping. Kids will be happy with just the jam, so they make a lovely, not-too-naughty addition to their lunchbox.

MAKES about 10　　**PREPARATION TIME** 20 minutes　　**COOKING TIME** 12 minutes

300 g (10½ oz/2 cups) self-raising flour
Pinch of salt
2 tablespoons caster (superfine) sugar
30 g (1 oz) chilled butter, chopped
200 ml (7 fl oz) milk, plus extra, to glaze
2½ tablespoons raspberry jam
Icing (confectioners') sugar, to dust
Thick (double/heavy) cream, to serve

1　Preheat the oven to 220°C (425°F/ Gas 7). Lightly grease a baking tray or line with non-stick baking paper.

2　Sift the flour and salt together into a medium mixing bowl and stir in the sugar. With your palms facing upwards, use your fingertips to rub in the butter until the mixture resembles fine breadcrumbs. Make a well in the centre.

3　Add almost all the milk and mix with a flat-bladed knife, using a cutting action, until the dough comes together in clumps. Mix to a soft dough, adding the remaining milk if necessary.

4　Use lightly floured hands to gently gather the dough, lift it onto a lightly floured work surface and knead very lightly and briefly to bring it together into a smooth ball. Use a lightly floured rolling pin to roll the dough out to 1 cm (½ inch) thick. Use a floured round 8 cm (3¼ inch) cutter to cut out scones, pressing straight down in the cutter and not twisting it. Gather the dough trimmings together and, without handling them too much, press out again to a 1 cm (½ inch) thickness and cut out more rounds. Use your fingertips to make an indentation on one side of each round (*pic 1*) and place a little jam in each indentation (*pic 2*). Brush the edges of the dough lightly with the extra milk, then fold the dough in half to make a semi-circle, covering the jam, then pinch the edges together (*pic 3*). Place the scones on the prepared tray, about 3 cm (1¼ inches) apart. Brush lightly with a little more milk.

5　Bake the scones for 12 minutes or until they are well risen, golden brown on top and sound hollow when tapped on the base. Serve warm, dusted with icing sugar and accompanied by thick cream.

1

2

3

TIP These scones are best eaten on the day they are baked.

Damper

This is the Australian version of soda bread. It was made by the stockmen known as swagmen or drovers, who travelled to remote areas of bushland for weeks or months at a time with only basic rations to cook with. Using everyday ingredients, limited utensils and a simple method, damper is the perfect example of a quick bread.

SERVES 8   **PREPARTATION TIME** 15 minutes   **COOKING TIME** 20-25 minutes

450 g (1 lb/3 cups) self-raising flour, plus extra, to dust
1–2 teaspoons sea salt
90 g (3¼ oz) unsalted butter, melted
125 ml (4 fl oz/½ cup) milk, plus extra, to glaze
Butter, to serve

1 Preheat the oven to 210°C (415°F/ Gas 6–7). Lightly grease a baking tray or line with non-stick baking paper.

2 Sift the flour and salt together into a bowl and make a well in the centre. Combine the butter, milk and 160 ml (5¼ fl oz) water and pour into the well in the flour mixture. Use a flat-bladed knife to stir until just combined.

3 Turn the dough out onto a lightly floured surface and knead for 20 seconds or until smooth. Place the dough on the prepared tray and press out to a 20 cm (8 inch) round.

4 Use a lightly floured large, sharp knife to score the dough into eight sections, about 1 cm (½ inch) deep. Brush with a little extra milk and dust with the extra flour.

5 Bake the damper for 10 minutes. Reduce the oven temperature to 180°C (350°F/Gas 4) and bake for a further 10–15 minutes or until it is risen, golden brown on top and sounds hollow when tapped on the base. Serve warm or at room temperature with butter.

TIPS If you prefer, you can make four small rounds instead of one large damper and slightly reduce the cooking time. Cut two slashes in the form of a cross on the top of each round.

Damper is best eaten on the day it is baked, or freeze in an airtight container for up to 8 weeks. Thaw at room temperature and then reheat wrapped in foil in an oven preheated to 160°C (315°F/Gas2-3) for 10-15 minutes.

Seeded rye damper

This quick, easy bread is great for lunchtime and makes a tasty accompaniment for soups and stews. The caraway seeds add another dimension, but you could substitute cumin seeds for a different flavour if you like. The use of rye flour gives the damper an earthy flavour.

SERVES 8   **PREPARATION TIME** 15 minutes   **COOKING TIME** 20 minutes

225 g (8 oz/1½ cups) self-raising
   flour
120 g (4¼ oz/1 cup) rye flour
2 teaspoons baking powder
Pinch of salt
30 g (1 oz) chilled butter, chopped
1½ teaspoons poppy seeds
1½ teaspoons caraway seeds
250 ml (9 fl oz/1 cup) milk,
   plus extra, to glaze
Butter, to serve

1   Preheat the oven to 220°C (425°F/ Gas 7). Lightly grease a baking tray or line with non-stick baking paper.

2   Sift the flours, baking powder and salt together into a bowl (*pic 1*). With your palms facing upwards, use your fingertips to rub in the butter until the mixture resembles fine breadcrumbs. Combine the seeds, reserve 2 teaspoons of the mixture and add the rest to the flour. Make a well in the centre.

3   Add almost all the milk and mix with a flat-bladed knife, using a cutting action, until the dough comes together in clumps (*pic 2*). Mix to a soft dough, adding the remaining milk if necessary.

4   Use lightly floured hands to gently gather the dough together, lift it onto a lightly floured work surface and knead very lightly and briefly to bring it together into a smooth ball. Pat the dough out to a round, 2.5 cm (1 inch) thick, and place on the prepared tray. Use a lightly floured large, sharp knife to deeply score the round of dough into 8 wedges, without cutting all the way through (*pic 3*). Brush lightly with the extra milk and then sprinkle with the reserved seed mixture.

5   Bake the damper for 20 minutes or until it is risen, golden brown on top and sounds hollow when tapped on the base. Serve warm or at room temperature with butter.

1

2

3

TIP This damper is best eaten on the day it is baked.

Cornbread

Before wheat replaced corn as a dominant crop in America, cornbread was a staple food that was served with just about everything. It's still popular as a comfort and convenience food, and is delicious served with soups, casseroles and barbecued meats.

SERVES 8–10   **PREPARATION TIME** 20 minutes   **COOKING TIME** 20 minutes

150 g (5½ oz/1 cup) plain
  (all-purpose) flour
2 teaspoons baking powder
190 g (6¾ oz/1 cup) polenta
2 tablespoons caster (superfine)
  sugar
1½ teaspoons salt
80 g (2¾ oz) unsalted butter,
  chopped
125 g (4½ oz) cheddar cheese,
  diced
1 large red chilli, chopped
1 egg, at room temperature,
  lightly whisked
250 ml (9 fl oz/1 cup) buttermilk
Butter, to serve (optional)

1   Preheat the oven to 200°C (400°F/ Gas 6). Brush a square 20 cm (8 inch) cake tin with melted butter to grease and lightly dust with flour.

2   Sift the flour and baking powder together into a large bowl. Stir in the polenta, sugar and salt. With your palms facing upwards, use your fingertips to rub in the butter until the mixture resembles fine breadcrumbs. Stir through the cheese and chilli *(pic 1)*.

3   Whisk together the egg and buttermilk. Add to the flour mixture and use a large metal spoon to stir until just combined *(pic 2)*. Spoon the mixture into the prepared tin and smooth the surface with the back of a spoon.

4   Bake the cornbread for 20 minutes or until light golden and a skewer inserted into the centre of the bread comes out clean *(pic 3)*. Leave in the tin for 5 minutes before turning out onto a wire rack. Serve warm or at room temperature, plain or spread with butter, if desired.

1

2

3

TIP This cornbread is best eaten on the day it is baked.

Banana bread

Once you start making this cafe-style banana bread, you'll find it hard to stop. It ticks every box: simple to make (it's a melt-and-mix recipe), perfect for any time of day, and wonderfully flavoursome, with just the right balance of banana, nuts and brown sugar.

SERVES 8–10 **PREPARATION TIME** 20 minutes **COOKING TIME** 50 minutes

335 g (11¾ oz/2¼ cups) plain (all-purpose) flour
1 teaspoon baking powder
¼ teaspoon bicarbonate of soda (baking soda)
3 large (about 200 g/7 oz each) ripe bananas, mashed (see tip) (pic 1)
2 eggs, at room temperature, lightly whisked
125 ml (4 fl oz/½ cup) vegetable oil
220 g (7¾ oz/1 cup, firmly packed) brown sugar
2 teaspoons natural vanilla extract
100 g (3½ oz) pecan or walnut halves, coarsely chopped

1 Preheat the oven to 180°C (350°F/ Gas 4). Lightly grease and flour a 10 x 20 cm (4 x 8 inch) loaf (bar) tin.

2 Sift the flour, baking powder and bicarbonate of soda together into a large bowl.

3 Put the mashed bananas, egg, oil, sugar and vanilla in a separate bowl and stir with a fork to combine well *(pic 2)*. Add the banana mixture to the flour mixture and stir with a large metal spoon until just combined. Stir in the pecans or walnuts. Pour into the prepared tin *(pic 3)* and smooth the surface with the back of a spoon.

4 Bake for 50 minutes or until a skewer inserted into the centre of the loaf comes out clean. Cool in the tin for 10 minutes, then turn out onto a wire rack to cool completely.

VARIATION

Chocolate and raisin banana bread: Replace 50 g (1¾ oz/⅓ cup) of the flour with 40 g (1½ oz/⅓ cup) unsweetened cocoa powder. Replace the brown sugar with 220 g (7¾ oz/ 1 cup) caster (superfine) sugar. Replace the pecans with 170 g (5¾ oz/1 cup) raisins and add 100 g (3½ oz/⅔ cup) chopped dark chocolate. Cook for 55–65 minutes.

1
2
3

TIPS You will need about 360 g (12¾ oz/1½ cups) mashed banana for this recipe.
   Keep in an airtight container for up to 3 days.
   To freeze, wrap well in plastic wrap, put in an airtight container or sealed freezer bag and freeze for up to 6 weeks.

Conversion charts

OVEN TEMPERATURE		
C	F	Gas
70	150	$\frac{1}{4}$
100	200	$\frac{1}{2}$
110	225	$\frac{1}{2}$
120	235	$\frac{1}{2}$
130	250	1
140	275	1
150	300	2
160	315	2–3
170	325	3
180	350	4
190	375	5
200	400	6
210	415	6–7
220	425	7
230	450	8
240	475	8
250	500	9

LENGTH	
cm	inches
2 mm	$\frac{1}{16}$
3 mm	$\frac{1}{8}$
5 mm	$\frac{1}{4}$
8 mm	$\frac{3}{8}$
1	$\frac{1}{2}$
1.5	$\frac{5}{8}$
2	$\frac{3}{4}$
2.5	1
3	$1\frac{1}{4}$
4	$1\frac{1}{2}$
5	2
6	$2\frac{1}{2}$
7	$2\frac{3}{4}$
7.5	3
8	$3\frac{1}{4}$
9	$3\frac{1}{2}$
10	4
11	$4\frac{1}{4}$
12	$4\frac{1}{2}$
13	5
14	$5\frac{1}{2}$
15	6
16	$6\frac{1}{4}$
17	$6\frac{1}{2}$
18	7
19	$7\frac{1}{2}$
20	8
21	$8\frac{1}{4}$
22	$8\frac{1}{2}$
23	9
24	$9\frac{1}{2}$
25	10
30	12
35	14
40	16
45	$17\frac{3}{4}$
50	20

WEIGHT	
g	oz
5	$\frac{1}{8}$
10	$\frac{1}{4}$
15	$\frac{1}{2}$
20	$\frac{3}{4}$
30	1
35	$1\frac{1}{4}$
40	$1\frac{1}{2}$
50	$1\frac{3}{4}$
55	2
60	$2\frac{1}{4}$
70	$2\frac{1}{2}$
80	$2\frac{3}{4}$
85	3
90	$3\frac{1}{4}$
100	$3\frac{1}{2}$
115	4
120	$4\frac{1}{4}$
125	$4\frac{1}{2}$
140	5
150	$5\frac{1}{2}$
175	6
200	7
225	8
250	9
280	10
300	$10\frac{1}{2}$
350	12
375	13
400	14
450	1 lb
500	1 lb 2 oz
550	1 lb 4 oz
600	1 lb 5 oz
700	1 lb 9 oz
800	1 lb 12 oz
900	2 lb
1 kg	2 lb 3 oz

LIQUID	
ml	fl oz
30	1
60	2
80	$2\frac{1}{2}$
100	$3\frac{1}{2}$
125	4
160	$5\frac{1}{4}$
185	6
200	7
250	9
300	$10\frac{1}{2}$
350	12
375	13
400	14
500	17
600	21
650	$22\frac{1}{2}$
700	24
750	26
800	28
1 L	35
1.25 L	44
1.5 L	52

Index

Published in 2013 by Murdoch Books Pty Limited.

Murdoch Books Australia
83 Alexander Street
Crows Nest NSW 2065
Phone: +61 (0) 2 8425 0100
Fax: +61 (0) 2 9906 2218
www.murdochbooks.com.au
info@murdochbooks.com.au

Murdoch Books UK Limited
Erico House, 6th Floor
93–99 Upper Richmond Road
Putney, London SW15 2TG
Phone: +44 (0) 20 8785 5995
Fax: +44 (0) 20 8785 5985
www.murdochbooks.co.uk
info@murdochbooks.co.uk

For Corporate Orders & Custom Publishing contact
Noel Hammond, National Business Development Manager
Murdoch Books Australia

Publisher: Anneka Manning
Designers: Susanne Geppert and Robert Polmear
Photographers: Louise Lister, Julie Renouf, George Seper,
  Jared Fowler
Stylists: Kate Nixon, Marie-Hélénè Clauzon, Jane Hann,
  Cherise Koch
Editors: Anna Goode, Melissa Penn
Project Editor: Martina Vascotto
Food Editors: Leanne Kitchen, Anneka Manning
Recipe Development: Sonia Greig, Leanne Kitchen, Cathie Lonnie,
Anneka Manning, Lucy Nunes
Home Economists: Grace Campbell, Dixie Elliot, Joanne Glynn,
Caroline Jones, Sharon Kennedy, Lucy Lewis, Sabine Spindler
  Allan Wilson
Production Manager: Karen Small

Text and Design © Murdoch Books Pty Limited 2012
Photography © Louise Lister and Murdoch Books Pty Ltd 2012

A cataloguing-in-publication entry is available from the catalogue
of the National Library of Australia at www.nla.gov.au.

A catalogue record for this book is available from the British Library.

Printed by 1010 Printing International Limited, China

The Publisher and stylist would like to thank Breville
(www.breville.com.au) for lending equipment for use
and photography.

IMPORTANT: Those who might be at risk from the effects of
salmonella poisoning (the elderly, pregnant women, young children
and those suffering from immune deficiency diseases) should
consult their doctor with any concerns about eating raw eggs.

OVEN GUIDE: You may find cooking times vary depending on
the oven you are using. For fan-forced ovens, as a general rule, set
the oven temperature to 20°C (35°F) lower than indicated in the
recipe.

MEASURES GUIDE: We have used 20 ml (4 teaspoon) tablespoon
measures. If you are using a 15 ml (3 teaspoon) tablespoon add an
extra teaspoon of the ingredient for each tablespoon specified.